Eleven Short Essays

★

Traumear

Paperback ISBN 978-0-244-99071-8

*

www.traumear.com

Index of titles

★ ★ ★

*

These essays were written over a period of several years and are not presented here in chronological order. They are research essays inasmuch as they break some new ground while they lean substantially on previous, larger essays. The essay 'The Power of Purpose' was written as an exercise in response to an essay competition. The others were penned on the spur of the moment when there was need of extra clarity on some topic.

*

Essay

An essay, for me, is an exploration of the unknown. New knowledge and clearer knowledge is the purpose of it. Even as I write an essay on what I mean by an essay, my mind is blank to begin with. I have a vague notion of an essay as an attempt, a trial, a trip into no-man's-land in the hope of being able to return smarter, better informed – but also more skilled.

But knowledge and skill go together in any case. Surely I am not alone in thinking that. What I know I can invest. So part of the essay is practical, is practice on the spot for applying what is being found out. A great deal of knowledge cannot come to us in any case except during the application of it. Even if I were to write an essay about horses or churches I would still be mainly interested in my developing attitude, in my enquiring spirit.

Is an essay necessarily a literary form? I ask myself, can I drag myself out of the dumps with it or bring myself down safely from a physical high? As I come to the point where I don't know what to say next, I can of course keep quiet but is it also possible for me to 'essay' to say something else? My knowledge has come to an end, I do not know how to go on, but now the essay comes into its own. I am not all that surprised that I have come to the end of my knowledge, there is not that much of it, however now I want to raid the larder. In all modesty and humility I accept that I have come to the end of my tether but the least thing I know is that if I go about it in a certain way I can now extend my knowledge. I have not been defeated by ignorance. That can only happen if my knowledge until now was egotistical. If, however, it was truthful, I should now be able to extend it, to add to it.

1

So an aspect of the essay is learning. How does one go about that, in this case? It seems to me that in order to be able to do that, one has to come to the task believing, or assuming, that an infinite amount of knowledge both exists, in reality, and is always available, to be gained and shared, by anyone who desires to gain and share it for the right reasons and for a good purpose. If suddenly the well seems to dry up, that is a misconception. One has to assume one is not lowering the bucket properly. One has to take the responsibility upon oneself.

*

I have to ask myself: Where does language come from? Here again I have this intuition that speech originates at the point where outward and inward awareness intersect and the essay allows me to define that point, to identify it and to demonstrate that this is in fact how it is. An essay would refresh for me my capacity for language and speech, would reconnect me with the root of the word, so to speak. Words don't float in the air, they spring from human perception.

*

So is the essay form a private affair? Can we think of it as intentionally subjective? That would haradly make sense. However if we place our individuality, correctly as I believe, beneath our communal personality, as support and resource, rather that on a pedestal by itself, then the essay-pursuit would have a reason that lies beyond it, and of that reason the writer of the essay would have to be aware.

What we have, then, is the essay as exploration, even exploitation, of individual knowledge, with the understanding that individual knowledge is no end in itself but it serves, eventually and in good time, the community, somehow. That locates it for the time being.

Meanwhile we might ask: What do we have a right to expect from, or as, 'individual knowledge'? Not everybody would agree that here, or there, something new is to be gained. It has to be new. It is new knowledge we have in mind. If the knowledge on offer is not new, we are on the wrong track with our essay. We insist that we want new knowledge and we have a hunch that we can get hold of it, by way of an essay; an essay like a foray into unfamiliar territory.

Which raises the point of legitimacy. Foray implies illegitimacy. This has to be consciously avoided. There is such a thing as illegitimate knowledge and, secretly observing our own present essay approach, we are grateful to have discovered this. It has all the earmarks of new knowledge. Comparatively new?

The only way the illegitimacy can be avoided is if we go about our task in the above mentioned spirit of individual knowledge, in the particular, to the general end of personal, communal use, application, investment. Individual knowledge sought as an end in itself, no matter how great the popular acclaim of the genius who seeks it and offers it for general consumption, is illegitimate. Notice the difference here. While individual knowledge is sought, the seeker must keep in mind why he is searching. What is his motivation? This motivation plays into the search process. If he blindly throws himself into his task, perhaps for no other reason than that it feels good to do so, he will come up with something, very likely. He may come up with a great deal, however it will be illegitimate. Then he irresponsibly offers that to others and allows the illegitimacy to bear fruit. It will bear fruit alright, but bad fruit.

The personal, communal motivation is therefore essential as the general purpose if the essayed knowledge is not to be gained blindly, illegitimately. Our essay shall not be a robbery, a case of breaking and entering and we shall have no truck with those who offer us the outcome or result of theft.

We recognize the stolen goods, don't we, by the way they draw attention to the thief. They point to him, and only other thieves will applaud. Sometimes the applause is deafening.

Back to our legitimate task. I say 'our', but really it is mine in the particular. I take you, the present reader, along as the one for whom I perform it.

*

It may come as a surprise that the essay suddenly loses itself in a mist of unknowing. For a while it all went as planned. The plan was a short one and the essay had thrown it up, so that the new knowledge appeared according to that plan, the plan that itself amounted to new knowledge.

But then the fields, and the trees behind them, and the hills behind those, all disappeared in a fog. The fog itself was invisible, one only knew it was there in faith, it must have been there, to hide all else, there was no question about it, about the faith fog, which itself too was knowledge.

The essay is now legitimated. No longer does the searcher for new knowledge seem to risk all. He knows who he is and he knows that by referring to himself he does not incriminate himself in the making of an empty gesture. Where there is faith, there is sound basis for being. The essay has worked its own springboard.

This is a stage through which every essay must be taken, the void followed by the basic faith. We will recognize that stage and we will not be put off, not be devastated by it and leap to fearful conclusions. Many a good essay began well but then was spoiled by this fear of the void, so that fear takes the place of faith and produces its frantic children.

If now in faith I refer to myself, I have nothing to worry about because my true being is substantial, in relation to my faith. When I refer to my true being in this present essay on the essay as a literary form I mean an infinity of possible knowledge which may be gained by me. An infinite crop stands ready to be harvested.

But of course my essay, anyone's essay, has a theme, a focus. I may write an essay on love, on the reading of books, on the art of true imitation. This is my thread through the labyrinth. How interesting! someone will say. I had no idea imitation, or love, could be so interesting. But of course the love- or imitation-related information is incidental. The interest-factor is not central to the issue. None of the new knowledge has been applied. The grain is harvested, threshed and stored, all that, but no bread is baked. The baking of the bread is beyond the essay and must remain so.

*

What is this new knowledge? Can it be talked about? Does one refer to it obliquely?

Call it fundamental knowledge, or faith knowledge. It cries out for application. Think of the legitimacy of it, or otherwise. That part will stay with us forever. It will come in handy on numerous occasions; do you see what I mean? A powerful human being has a lot of new, fundamental knowledge. In a way it is like a tool kit or a bank balance, except that even the mere possession of it radiates from a person like confidence, like dependability, but also like a danger to the half-hearted approach by anyone to reality. So you mustn't act all surprised when they come for you and gang up on you, demanding to know the basis of your confidence, the reason for your strength. Is it not a good sign, that they come to pester you and inadvertently call you unfriendly names?

5

I believe that the true essay cannot be written by anyone who has not found his own centre. If I don't know that I am, I am bound, for example, to exert my will or to exercise my intellect and this is fine as far as it goes if it does go somewhere and hopefully in the end, by design or default, the centre will have been discovered and the world will no longer be the fragment it seemed. But an essay of will or an essay of intellect will be presumptuous or arbitrary, possibly both. The essay you write, in that case, cannot give you your initial piece of faith knowledge. The true essay you read can. This is because the essay gives evidence, it testifies inadvertently. We read the essay and perhaps we say: How can this be possible? Considering that this works, as it obviously does, what are the implications? Evidently someone here is who he is, otherwise he would not be able to make these moves, to ask these questions, to come up with these goods. There is more to it than acrobatics. My intellect on its own can manage those, to astonish, for applause. All the same certain unusual moves are obviously being made, extraordinary connections too. Gracious me, I have never seen the likes! How it affects me! I try to control it with my will alone but lose it. Then I try to analyze it with my intellect alone but the process is endless. Beyond the futility and the impotence, I am still moved. Confronting this affection with only a part of me, I am defeated, time and again. I lose or am lost. The influence of the essay is carried to where not my intellect or my will but I myself might be. If all goes well I discover that I am.

*

The technique of the essay is worth studying. Take the parallel technique. What you have in mind is something you know. Now you let your mind search for something like it. You employ the known quantity as imprint until your novel notion catches on like a fly on sticky paper. What you have then is not necessarily worthless. Mere novelty for its own sake is worthless. But what if you refer it to yourself?

Let me give you a example. I begin with a familiar notion: The individual human being coming out of and away from the private/public sector of consciousness and developing personality. I see that as one of the central themes of growing ethical awareness. Now I come along on behalf of my essay and try for a parallel structure that will open new fields of interest for me. The experience of moods comes to mind and the recognition of the difference between so-called good and bad moods, attachment to the former and censorship of the latter, sometimes long before the need, in the interest of the work progress, for the repression of mood at all is given due consideration.

The parallel structure here is this business of getting caught up in good and bad mood as though that might deliver us from ourselves and into the realm of personality, when we should in fact repress our mood, good or bad, creating thereby a mystic union of oneself with the world.

This efficacy towards mystic union is new knowledge, gained by means of parallel technique within the practical confines of an essay. The repression can be set in motion anytime, before or after the separation of good and bad moods, though only rarely do we even notice our mood experience unless it has been tainted by pleasure or pain.

*

Take instead the technique of extrapolation.

By way of our essay we have conquered a bit of territory. Shall we not now extend it? No need to make reason our God. For present purposes, why not have a go with the results of the previous example of parallel technique: if something were to be gained from the repression of mood experience then

7

why not demonstrate and document just such an instant of that? Once again, our intention will not be primarily but only secondarily to increase the realm or amount of the physical. The principle of the essay is the storage of metaphysical knowledge.

Mood, then, once recognized, can be repressed, even prior to its occurrence, due to our own agency of course, as 'good' or 'bad' mood. Such repression shall not be an act of will but I myself do the repressing. I do it by saying to it: 'I' rather than 'you'.

Once again, what must be obvious is that *I* exist rather than not I but my ego. What the ego represses, ends up in a foul mess, fodder for the psychoanalyst, who undoes, at best, the abuse of the ego but leaves the ego intact, this time not to re-press, but perhaps to elevate, which amounts to the same.

What is it that happens to my mood, or to my good or bad mood, as I repress it, saying: I, not you?

Now the essay comes into its own, because otherwise I have not a clue. I take care to refrain from pretending that I know. I have to be doing what I intend to describe. I can only begin to describe what I am actually doing.

Repression of mood clarifies perception. That must be set down at the start. At the same time, mood is not properly iden-tified except under pressure. So it would seem to make sense that one should now and again make a point of asserting one-self inwardly, of holding the truth of one's being. Any particu-lar mood, necessarily good or bad, will then slip into the focus of clarified perception and become available for repression.

While I hold the truth that I am, this truth may repeatedly be assailed by one mood or another, whereupon I may just as re-peatedly insist, inwardly, that I am. Moods tend to make me behave as though I were not I but rather a mood-ridden ego. This cannot be rationally expressed.

As I repeatedly insist that I am, against the onset of moods, I become capable. If no moods assail me I am even then capable and may act.

So it seems that we have a choice here. We can either be in a mood, moody, or else capable of action. As I repress my mood I become capable of a certain kind of action – or rather not, precisely not of a certain kind of it, but of action itself, as such, pure and simple. We might call it original creative action. This is what our essay teaches us at the moment. It has shown us how to arrive at original creative action by way of mood repression and it has allowed us to demonstrate that we can successfully repress mood and moods by insisting that <u>we</u> are and not the mood ego.

But does this mean that 'moods are bad'? That is the sort of question one is asked. Besides, repression itself has a 'bad press'. The fashion is all for 'letting it out', 'bringing it out', for expression, not repression.

Let's just compare emotion and 'mood'. Actually there is no such thing as mood. There is a mood, bad or good, but not mood as such. We speak, latterly, of 'mood swings'. One may be 'moody', experience 'moodiness'. Emotion on the other hand, emotion as such, not yet particular, is quite conceivable.

Before we get ourselves into too much bother with finite definitions, let us admit that most of us are familiar with 'depression'. When I say 'depression', hardly anyone assumes I mean a lowering in the level of the ground or in the icing of the Christmas cake. It seems to be a very contemporary inward state, an emotional state, perhaps, or mental and spiritual.

So it occurs to me that unless I repress my moods I get depressed. That is it in a nutshell. Without looking any further at the difference between moods, humours, emotions, tempers, passions etc., it makes good sense to me to act on the basis of this connection between voluntary repression and debilitating depression.

Possibly moods are, by definition, under some sort of pressure in any case. Hypothetically, even a 'good mood' shows evidence of containment and confinement. He is 'in a good frame of mind' we say, meaning something like a 'good mood'. On the other hand, there is the suggestion that he may just be lucky to be in a good mood and any moment it may tip to the other side.

Our essay is taking us not only into unfamiliar territory but into an unfamiliar jungle, into lush growth. Our primary goal is not knowledge of moods but knowledge pure and simple, which gets stored for future use. This jungle is just what the doctor ordered. An essay is somewhat scientific, somewhat philosophical too, but primarily experimental, a leap out of the dark into what we believe will be light and then *is* light. We are not to arrive at any conclusions about anything, in our present case not even about the essay, since it is an essay we write – about the essay practice and form and about why we might choose to write an essay.[1]

All the same, moods and pressure seem to go together somehow. If I do not apply the pressure myself but wait for it to be done to me, then that is unpleasant. If I am serous about it being actual repression that is required, then I am suggesting, I suppose, that these moods were once under pressure, slipped out from under it, to my detriment it seems, and now need to be 'pressed again, repressed'. They existed perhaps under one sort of pressure and now a different sort is to be ap-

---

[1] The creative composer of music, the serious painter too, may proceed in this fashion and for the purpose I describe here.

plied. That would make sense, in terms of human growth and development.

It looks like this now: Moods are nicely contained, like law-abiding citizens and we barely notice them. In fact it might be alright to say they don't even exist until they slip the leash, so to speak, and then we become moody, blue, over optimistic, down in the mouth, elated – depressed. We can speculate on what they amount to, if anything, prior to their existence. Do they appear out of nothing? The law-abiding citizen is overlooked until he commits a crime and then it turns out it was something that more or less came over him, he forgot himself. That is how the good citizen looks at it. It would not occur to him, that he himself can be anything other than good until this unfortunate thing happens to him, as he slides into embezzlement, bribery, perhaps even into mayhem and murder, as one can read in the tabloids. Once it has happened to him and he gets over his surprise he may actually insist he is not responsible because, after all, it happened to him. So he goes on actually to initiate that sort of thing in the future, it felt so good when it 'came over him – or he may review his definition of himself as a 'good man' and take the responsibility for what happened to him. If that can happen to me, he says, what are the implications for me in terms of initiative, choice, self-satisfaction etc? What does that tell me about 'how I am' when that sort of thing can happen to me?

I think we can agree that moods happen to us and that what matters is what we do afterwards, if anything. If we repress them, they do not end up where they were and we ourselves are not as we were prior to the existence of those moods.

Which reminds me: Since my moodiness has got me into trouble a few times, I become naturally cautious in a fearful sort of way and then you might say that I unintentionally repress them. I don't think much of that, because it reminds me of 'the unconscious', which has never made much sense to me. How can we do anything unintentionally? No, once again it happens to us. If the good citizen is afraid of committing another crime, it makes no good sense for him to become 'intentionally law-abiding'. Intention and fear only mix when we know what we fear, not when we're afraid on reflex, accidentally. Well, that goes without saying. Intentional repression is not the same as accidental repressions. What I question is: should the accidental variety be called repression at all. If one moment I am peevish, cross and in the dumps and the next moment, let's say after someone has shouted at me, I am just plain scared and nothing else, it would make more sense to say that my mood has been annihilated, murdered even and that I then walk around with the corpse of it in me, that sort of thing.

By the intentional repression of a mood I mean something else. I mean the kind of transformation that could nearly be called a transubstantiation. But I am not happy with that either. When I feel mournful and downcast, I can do something about it but it can be profitable. When I say: 'I myself, not this mood!' I do not have to do that hatefully. We have already noticed how the self-assertive or morbid ego can slip in here if we are not careful. It would seem reasonable that we advocate not at all a negative but a kindly predisposition towards our moods, whether they originate in us or occur due to infection.

*

So we have a slightly better notion now of what a research essay is and of what our reasons might be for undertaking one – in whatever medium, for that matter. A practical demonstration of it has done it for us.

* * * * *

12

Matter

Matter is particles of resistance.

How do we understand this? The first question that naturally arises is: resistance to what?

On reflection I have to say: resistance to growth.

Next question? We know that growth implies growth against. In other words nothing organically grows in a vacuum or alongside everything else growing a the same rate in the same direction. It grows against 'this and that', which is either not growing, or not growing in the same direction or at the same rate.

We mustn't forget meanwhile that the growth we mean is always bound by an individual intelligence. It does not occur, arbitrarily or by chance. Whatever and whoever grows does so from within its or his need to do so.

I am mainly interested in how, why and when I grow, and what I understand about that allows me to say something hopefully helpful about another being's growth.

So what interests me here about this organic or 'physical' growth is that matter has to be available for growth to succeed.

The term 'successful growth' implies that matter is in the process of being overcome.

If we limit our definition of matter to 'particles of resistance' rather than just plain resistance, we might wonder would it be useful to enquire about the nature of those particles, are there different ones, do they resist in different ways that would be helpful for us to know ahead of time. In other words, does it make sense to study these particles? Should we take any interest in them at all, and if not, what is the point of thinking in terms of particular matter in the first place?

Well, on one hand we need to know that matter is finite and that every particle is finite and therefore in no way gradable. We cannot identify such a thing as individual particles. At the same time, the resistant matter is endless. Matter in itself, taken by itself and independently from a growing being, is finite but in terms of a growing being there is an endless number of resisting particles and those we overcome by growing make room and time for new or other ones.

Matter is like the ladder we can scale until we have reached the height we are born with to each.

The progress a successfully growing being makes in terms of contribution to community does not depend at all on the nature of particular material resistance.[1] We have to put out of our mind the notion that some beings are 'harder done by' than others, or that some have an easier time of it − due to the nature or size of resistance met. To each his own appropriate burden for progress sand success. Looking beyond or outside this peculiar burden of resistance, peculiar to a given being, falsifies.

The main question finally, I suppose, is how does our understanding of matter as particle resistance help us to grow more successfully?

Let's look at some of the hindrances to successful growth.

An important one is a joyless existence; in other words a lack of joy. We become miserable, negative, critical. 'What's the matter with you,' someone will ask, little realizing he's put his finger directly on the problem, namely, we are not identifying matter, we are not dealing with matter as matter, as particles of resistance, but we are mistaking it for something dead,

---

[1] This throws up the exciting notion that every being, whether human, animal, vegetal etc. contributes to its community of beings. Any interest we take in this is most rewarding.

and that depresses us. What we need to do therefore is root around in our constitution on the look-out for this matter which we assume is dead when it isn't really dead but we do not recognize it, in truth, as particles of resistance to be overcome.

Another hindrance to successful growth might be energetic arrogance. During a joyless existence we lie down under matter and neglect to confront it, while during energetic arrogance we completely ignore matter as matter, accusing and abusing it. We walk all over it in hobnail boots and vow there is no such thing.

It amounts to the same, whether we neglect to overcome it or insist there is nothing to overcome. What it amounts to is lack of successful growth.

Extinction and hypertrophy for a long time have been – or rather are – the curses of modern life. Modern man strives to be immaterial and does this either as a materialist, not overcoming material resistance but making a (carnal) thing out of it, (recently again by building monstrous tools such as the Large Hadron Collider, so as to be able to torture particles and to study their painful reactions) or as a spiritualist, pretending there is really no such thing as matter and as a consequence setting up spirit indiscriminately or identifying with it impersonally.

Initially, therefore, we do well to identify matter, as particularly resistance to our wish to grow. Do we wish to grow? If we do, we can proceed to the second rung of the ladder. What is preventing us from growing successfully? Let us ask ourselves what the matter is. Whatever comes up needs to be overcome and can be overcome.

In our arrogance, our hypertrophic achievement, our supererogatory behaviour, we do not with to grow. Neither do we wish to grow while we court extinction.

So before we wonder what the matter is we really need to establish our wish to grow, because this organic growth doesn't work mechanically or accidentally. We have to know what we're about.

Let's just add the following co-ordinates: that we successfully grow towards oneness, wholeness and fullness. They are concepts, images or symbols for us, depending on who or how we are.

You may well have reason to wish for any one or more of these three and if you do, why not realize that you will attain to them – not magically, by will or intellect alone, (or in a puff of smoke) but by way of successful growth.

The wish to grow, let's remind ourselves, is usually hampered by one thing or another and we consider it worthwhile to view this 'something' as particular matter. How we think about this obstruction will make it easy, difficult or impossible for us to overcome it.

Take the way to make it impossible first. We pit ourselves against this material obstruction energetically, hoping thereby to conquer it, to negate it by sheer force of contradiction. We oppose it mightily. What happens is that we sheer off on one side or the other, on the side of blood, sweat and tears or on the side of guilt and shame. So much for that. We end up defeated or depleted, in spirit or in the flesh.

Next we look at how to make it difficult for ourselves. We try to interpret the obstruction. We want at least to make sense of it so that we know what we're up against, which is, of course, entirely unnecessary and a waste of strength. Nonetheless it gives us the satisfaction of having pitted ourselves against a worthy enemy. Shortly afterwards we meet the same enemy, unconquered, in some other guise.

It becomes easy and effective as soon as we remind our-selves that indeed we do wish to grow and we cannot grow except against some resistance – of which we need to know nothing except that it resists and that it is tailored for our em-ployment. The obstruction is conquered bit by bit, (particle by particle) more or less playfully, not because we want rid of it but because we wish to grow, knowing that growth is increase over and against. We do not allow ourselves to get side-tracked by the resistance, neither seductively nor for the sheer pleasure of control and this too is easy because we know our priority, which is to grow successfully.

So matter is particles of resistance and without it we would be lost. Without matter we would not be able to grow. If we want to grow successfully we must have a true notion of mat-ter, otherwise we create difficulties or impossibilities for our-selves.

One way of expressing this true notion of growth is as par-ticles of resistance. This is a philosophic expression of it, so we can, from it, in accordance with the nature of philosophy, (contemporary and creative, not merely traditional-intellectual philosophy) extrapolate any number of meaningful and there-fore helpful notions.

What matters is whatever inhibits our growth and therefore offers the possibility for further growth.

Our perception of such inhibitions must be contemporary and in the light of day, in other words concrete and not ab-stract, or absent-minded, or dreamy, or in our mind alone, or in our feelings, emotions or passions alone. Sometimes we first have to work our way through to contemporary perception, so that we do not come into conflict with matter, which happens accidentally, alas, all too often.

The thing is, if we do not want to grow we come into conflict with matter. Spiritualists solve this predicament conveniently. They argue matter away, assuming they can avoid painful growth with impunity. However that doesn't really work, does it. We can argue matter out of existence only for a while and then the directly proportionate conflict is upon us and we haven't a clue as to what happened or why. (e.g. the pure spirit we have groomed grows up and disowns us, to our immense chagrin!)[1]

If we want to grow we will grow. This is like saying: 'Ask and you will receive.'

If we want to grow and are able to perceive here and now, matter will occur to us in quanta of resistant particles which we welcome as steps in growth.

If we come into conflict with matter, this is painful and the pain is a mercy because it let's us know that we need to look to our behaviour, both of mind and body.

*

Quanta of resistant particles are imagined to an extent. here we put a face on something that bothers us. I am tired. my mother-in-law is a pain. that sort of thing once we do that we do well to take special care not to ignore that we ourselves are responsible or that face or aspect and that it is not real. The wish to grow successfully must now include a degree of de-construction. (I only suppose I am tired and must not expect sleep to do me good. My mother-in-law is not really a pain., I am making a mistake, best not to criticize her.) usually any allocation of blame is an attempt to rid ourselves of matter rather than to validate it. Or we feel shame but allow ourselves to be persuaded that it does not exist, or should not exist, that

---

[1] When Faust, in Goethe's work of that name, finally likens himself to the pure spirit he has identified, he hears him say: "Compare yourself to the spirit you can grasp, not to me!" and he sinks back in the despair out of which is born his desire for the fast solution, called Mephistopheles.

18

there is really no justification for it – in which case we forfeit an opportunity for growth.

It appears that by thinking in terms of matter we can add a shortcut to how we deal with what troubles and afflicts us. We avail ourselves of that common denominator. Think of it as yet another way of coping strongly and successfully, as contemporary human beings, in the modern world.

The wish or the intention to grow, either one, it makes no difference: that is the other side of the equation. Our awareness of ourselves as physical (not merely carnal or purely spiritual) beings allows us periodically to persuade ourselves of our organic, human need to grow – and therefore to take advantage of material resistance – which resistance does not prevent us from growing but rather it affords us, again and again, opportunities for further work-related growth.

*

Material resistance accumulates to the extent and degree that we are not aware of it – that is the other part to keep in mind. We have already recognized that if we plough ahead with our external or internal (not inward and outward) business, resistance accumulates 'in our absence' as it were. The moment we relax, this load lands on us – as an unfortunate experience or as an illness. Unforeseeable, we say. Yet had we paid proper attention, we would have noticed the material resistance and taken advantage of it in a growth-related manner a lot sooner. We could call it this accumulation of material resistance our *organism*[1] and we are aware of it to an extent or totally unaware of it. Fatigue, guilt, anxiety are organismic. Also haste, speed, all careless behaviour.

---

[1] Jesus of Nazareth, who seems to have know about matter, referred to it as a cross. If we are up for our resurrection we lift up our cross and follow him or else wait for him.

This name (organism, organismic) helps to keep us in mind of our organic being which is under duress to the extent and dimension of this organism – which is a thing, (a myth), not a being. The modern sciences like to study organisms because scientists promise themselves manipulative satisfaction, which merely blinds them, however, to the reality of growth, to the lively benefits of development and evolution. When they speak of organisms, they may not know or admit it but they have in mind extinct beings or things, which do not grow, as we know, and in the meantime they make no acquaintance with the organism of individual human being, which can only be known by what we might call the host individual. We find ourselves in the realm, here, of what we must all learn and do for ourselves. Looking after our evolution is our own business and no one can do it for us.[1] So we can imagine the organism[2] that gets in our way and which must be understood as growth-potential. It hinders our happiness, our having fun, our static existence, our penchant for dying. We have cause to be glad,[3] exceedingly glad and reason to be grateful for it. It crops up when we proceed too far or too fast in some particular direction or when we are not active enough to 'stop the rot'.

*

Matter countervails. Our understanding of this validates our progress. Strong, valid growth depends on a correct approach to material resistance. The material resistance we ex-

---

[1] Only think how much time and effort is invested by us when we try to remove these organismic burdens from others without first helping them understand that these are aids to developmental and evolutionary growth.

[2] We can learn, gradually, to think properly of an organism as a condition rather than as a being of some sort, as we deconstruct this particular extinct-scientific term.

[3] In fact by "being exceedingly glad" we deal sensibly with every organismic condition. Understandably those whose priorities are survival, happiness, fun, static existence and a penchant for dying are not interested in resurrectional growth.

perience relates proportionately to the quality of our development and quantitatively to our evolution. There is greater jubilation in heaven over a reformed sinner than over a righteous man. When we have good reason to climb a mountain we will make it easier for ourselves if we absorb any arduous reaction we experience. Any work we do gets harder the less we appreciate any difficulty we encounter. We are healthy to the extent that we destroy sickness but we are well while we respect illness as a merciful reminder, which means that health is static but wellbeing is lively. Sometimes it takes us to be in some extremity before we can make a breakthrough into such areas of wisdom.

*

It is no use telling us that we should cooperate with matter. In Goethe's 'Faust', the main character of that thoroughly modern tragedy, confesses, and displays, his modernity by responding to his frustration with magic. How does matter appear to him now? As Mephistopheles, who defines himself as:

„ ... ein Teil des Teils der anfangs alles war ... ein Teil von jener Kraft, die stets das Böse will und stets das Gute schafft ... der Geist der stets verneint."

" ... a part of the part that was all at the start ... a part of that strength that ever wants evil and ever produces the good .. the spirit that ever negates."

We see here, in mythic representation, not only a parallel to what we in this essay mean by matter but also what happens to matter when we get caught up in magic. The modern dualistic preoccupation with good versus evil vitiates human evolution, persuades us to conceive of the hindrance to progress as something that needs to be removed or destroyed so that happiness may blossom, meanwhile becoming involved in enormous labours that end in guilt and delusion. We cannot help but feel compassion for the modern Faust when, at the end of his life, he utters these heart-breaking words:

„Noch hab' ich mich ins Freie nicht gekämpft.
Könnt ich Magie von meinem Pfad entfernen,
Die Zaubersprüche ganz und gar verlernen,
Stünd' ich, Natur, vor dir ein Mann allein,
Da wär's der Mühe wert, ein Mensch zu sein."

Not yet have I fought my way into freedom.
Could I clear magic from my path,
Unlearn all spells and incantations;
If I could face nature as a solitary man,
Then it would be worth the effort to be a human being.

(Faust II, lines 11403-11407)

Perhaps even more are we moved near the end of that poetic tragedy, prior to the apotheosis, when Faust goes blind and realizes he knows nothing of care and compassion. Even now, as he dies, he deludes himself over his alleged accomplishments and mistakes the noise made by those who dig his grave for the start to his ambitious plan to reclaim land from the sea, supposedly so as to accommodate room for more human settlement. The sea he experiences as matter which must be pushed back, resisted. One gets the impression he would really prefer to be rid of the sea altogether. – Modern man wants to shrug off his cross, this irritating 'matter'. Also what counts for him is the mighty achievement of 'the human spirit', while the benefits to humanity are really humanistic justifications for the pleasure he gets from exercising his naked willpower. Do we ourselves not know this pleasure all too well?

*

So much of the tragedy of the modern age is contained in that work! The preoccupation with the fallacious shortcut, the failed entrance via the back-door to freedom; the misconcep-

22

tion of nature as essentially objective; the pride in solitary independence; the emphasis on effort, as if free human being could be gained by force.

As contemporary men we learn to view matter as convivial. He coexists with it, communally, on the friendliest of terms. It really amounts to our ‚helpmeet', in a certain sense. It helps us again and again to ‚meet our maker' if we are in danger of straying or of overstepping the mark. Tellingly, when Faust has entered the eternal realm, matter becomes helpful, appreciative, is imagined for us by the author as particularly maternal – ‚Mater Gloriosa,, ‚heilige Büßerinnen', (holy female penitents), including Gretchen, whom he has harmed and who pleads for him – and finally the eternally feminine, das Ewig-Weibliche, that 'draws us anon', is mentioned. Is it not almost as if Goethe, like Jesus of Nazareth before him, imagined the union of spirit and matter as groom and bride?

*

Right away I have a mild headache, and after half an hour I feel I ought to emphasize how what is required now is more like a giving in to the evolutionary growth impulse within me and 'an exceedingly glad' cooperation with it, rather than an effort of resisting or a declining into self-pity. So at such times as when we notice some material impediment, it seems best to bring to mind as soon as possible that we are naturally urged to develop or to evolve and that what counts now is that we take advantage of that and relax into a cooperation with our maker rather than feeling we have to initiate some ambitious process. Or let us simply say that, especially with the onset of our resurrection, we grow and sometimes it hurts, at which time we do well to agree to grow, because evidently we have either caused an impediment or allowed one to arise – it makes little difference which. And it will not be held against us. Should I say that we have faith in our resurrection and that at times we need to have extra faith in it? There are so many cultures and traditions from which to choose. Let no one insist on his own version but simply say how he sees sit and what works for him. That is what counts and what we have a right to ask from one another. I will let no one persuade me that I was not raised from among the dead and that I am not participating in my ongoing resurrection. It is up to me whether I believe that Jesus *is* the resurrection. And if the dead insist on giving me trouble because of what I say, then all I can add is: That is precisely what I was led to expect. At the same time I know that this is one way of putting it. Another way would be to say that the law of development and evolution, which is to say of growth, is engraved on my heart, which makes sense to me as a Gentile.

*

So in the last analysis, it would seem to make little sense to say that we should wish to grow or intend to grow since we grow in any case – either straight or crooked. So what, then; is matter merely a sign that we have inhibited growth? That matter is sin or the effect of our sin? In that case, if it helps us to think like that, a thoroughgoing repentance is as important as exceeding gladness. A mature contemporary man never ceases from offering his life for those who are still young and for those adults who are immature.

We do well to remember that growth is not separate from works. The matter is what we grow against. It is presented to us gratis. We more or less rise to the occasion – and that is where the pain may come in, to help us identify the most judicious, the most gratifying way forward. It is not the growth that is intentional but the work. We might even speak of positive and negative matter, depending on whether it attracts or directs us. And of dark matter when it tempts us?

Perhaps it is best simply to ask our god to deliver us from evil.

* * * * *

24

Notes on the Efficacy of Suffering

March 2016

If we think of god as creator, we right away also think of ourselves as creative, and therefore, as conjointly with god, responsible for all creatures. However creatures are not beings, and where beings are imagined we are bound to see god as love, not as creator.

Why should we not think when we wish to think and imagine when it suits us to imagine: an apple is edible, beautiful and also the fruit of a tree. I see no contradiction. Thought and imagination are not at war. However they must be at war when thought is not clear and imagination not distinct.

In order to clarify our thought we need only to wait until we are ready to communicate it. The communication of our thought is bound to be clear and we are the judges responsible for deciding whether our thought is ready for communication.

As for our imagination, its distinction depends entirely on the lack of any admixture of pictures. As soon as we picture something for any other reason than practical manipulation we interfere to that extent with our imagination. And imagination does, by the way, tend to expression and incline to presentation.

There is no reason why thought and imagination should not always be conjoined, or why our love should not always be creative. A deplorable error of our existence is this confusion of images with pictures and of thoughts with ideas. In fact when we go so far astray as to picture ideas we do not gather but we scatter and our works become both haphazard and offensive.

*

In order to understand the efficacy of suffering we need clear thought and distinct imagination. Pain is phenomenal, and therefore indicative. Once we appreciate this single fact, we should be well on our way to the acquisition of suffering as the first and foremost ability and skill that is required for creative living.

The loneliness that comes along with prolonged pain and the concentration upon individuality that characterizes acute pain indicates the source of healing. We should not assume that our initial reaction to pain, which is always a kind of fear, is anything other than what one would expect. However this fear would merely alert us to an external cause of injury. This is usually a minor issue. Much of course depends on the environment in which we find ourselves. External injury teaches us to be more careful in the future.

What interests me in this present study is the connection between suffering and healing. When we suffer, we take upon us some pain for a purpose. There is more to suffering than endurance. When we put up with pain, we have given up hope. When we struggle against pain, we aggravate the affliction. When we kill pain we admit we are, for the moment, at our wits' end.

There is nothing shameful in being at our wits' end. What we gain, when we kill pain, is a new start, a fresh look at things; in other words, a breathing space.

*

Next I should like to take a look at what it means to heal.

We can never return to a previous state. We either grow or we fall behind. Growth implies a rising to completion, wholeness and perfection. We grow in stages. Each stage implies a momentary setback, during which time pain is involved. If the pain is suffered, healing succeeds and growth proceeds. If the pain is killed we may well mend but there is not growth.

The breathing-space is an incalculable blessing. It has been referred to as a 'shortening of the days', in a wider context, and the emphasis is on us, that during that breathing-space we might re-establish our ability to suffer and our willingness to heal.

Healing as the result of suffering is really a life-long process, since we are not interested only in our own wholeness but also in the wholeness of the members of our community. Compassionately we adopt their pain. (This is a spiritual act.) We suffer it vicariously, so that as we are healed of their affliction, they too are healed and may participate in growth as they continue to rise out of the disadvantageously compromised aspects of their being. At another time they may do this for us. By suffering one another's shortfalls, setbacks and handicaps we heal one another.

*

As infants and as little children we are whole. During our youth we are liable to accumulate hardships and hindrances which may well cause us pain with the onset of maturity when the responsibility for successful growth is placed in our hands. So even if we have not yet actually caused ourselves any harm, through adult misdemeanour or negligence, we may nonetheless be in need of healing. However once we set out upon our maturity, no matter how holy we seem to ourselves to be, the work that necessarily comes along with maturation implies compassion, at least for those in our community who are in pain. Wholeness during our maturity is therefore to be achieved day after day. Compassion we have causes us to be less than whole but at the end of the day we are whole again and we have grown. For example, we have become more compassionate.

Holiness, sainthood really make no sense except as a popular fantasy promulgated mostly by those who assume they suffer when they are in pain. However being in pain is in truth

27

quite the opposite to suffering, as we soon enough discover when we try to have compassion with those who insist on remaining in pain because they realize somehow that suffering implies the distinction of the self from one's personhood and requires the choice of the latter over the former. Melancholy can readily turn into a choice to remain in pain and the unwillingness to suffer then shows up quite explicitly when a queer satisfaction is gained from a demand for a compassion. Such demanded compassion is rarely forthcoming.

When we are whole we have no wishes and no desires. Neither do we lack anything that we suppose might give us greater joy or satisfaction. What is more, we know that we are whole and we understand that being whole is not the purpose of our being. What matters is that we cannot be truly compassionate unless we are whole, so it stands to reason that we do not desire or wish to be compassionate.

True compassion, as we can see now, is spontaneous. We find ourselves being compassionate. It happens to us and we are glad that it does. For those who know what it means to be whole, true compassion is the only real happiness.

When we are compassionate we help others to suffer their pain and therefore to heal.

Now we know for sure that this cannot be faked. Since compassion is spontaneous, we cannot reasonably hope to gain anything from being compassionate. However we can gain a great deal – in fact we can gain real happiness – by choosing to suffer.

Even in the absence of pain we can choose to suffer. In the case of pain, suffering is more of a decision than a choice. However in the absence of pain – and of course even of the fear of pain and of death – our suffering may perhaps be an attitude, or an approach – or even an outlook.

Needless to say, pain is much less likely to surprise us if we have for some time chosen to suffer. If someone asks: How can I choose to suffer without suffering this or that? then we merely have to point them to the possibility – and certainly to the practicability – of suffering as an *attitude*, an *outlook* or an *approach*.

That may not be enough. We may actually have to set an example of what we mean.

1. So an *attitude* of suffering involves the imagination of all things and of the world in general as under sentence of death, while at the same time we think of all beings and of endless world as in spirit and reality perfected. This is not quite the attitude of seeing how something is in comparison to how it might be but somewhat similar. During the attitude of suffering we sustain that tension between fact and possibility, between the present situation and the underlying truth – that is to say, to the extent of any such tension and to the limit of our ability to sustain it.

Whether we see suffering now as an attitude, an outlook or an approach, it is work. So for example the aforementioned tension we sustain allows a creative capacity and potential energy to build up in ourselves which eventually ends in compassion.

This then gives us at least some insight into what suffering amounts to and how we want to go about it if we want to be capable of true compassion and be really happy.

*

2. Now if we imagine human beings, and all other beings through human beings, as always influenced by merciful love and then we think of how we ourselves might in fact be such human beings, who are at once influenced by love even as we

ourselves love other beings, then we gain insight into suffering as an *approach*.

This can of course be quite stressful work because we do not readily take to being loved mercifully. This is because mercy is good for us whether we like it and understand it or not. Also the loving we ourselves do has to be learned so that we do not confuse it with kindness and fondness. To the extent that we do confuse it we also mistake the effects on ourselves of merciful love, which may involve us then in stressful situations which, in turn, we do well to approach by suffering compassionately.

The emphasis during this approach is on ourselves to keep up to the mark. The merciful loving we ourselves need to do is bound to involve us in unpleasantnesses and inconveniences for which we do well to be as ready as possible, though absolutely ready we can never be. As soon as compassion becomes possible for us, however, every difficulty is eased and problems are dissolved.

So once again, this time in the case of suffering as an approach, we gain insight both into the work that is involved and the compassion that results.

*

Before I continue, with suffering as an outlook, let me just compare suffering, as a thought conception, to offering. When we show ourselves willing to suffer we offer ourselves as bearers of pain. You might say that we offer our services as healers. It is an offer that certainly becomes apparent in our attitude, so we have to be careful that we are not abused by those who merely seek to offload their troubles so that they can carry on with their trivial and trivializing existence. So this is why we are smart to go to some length in our understanding of what suffering, for ourselves and for others, amounts to and also what it does not amount to.

It is, therefore, not a question at all of a balance between thought and imagination but rather a case of care taken so that neither thought nor imagination fall behind, nor that one becomes independent from the other.

This is why true compassion is so rare for us moderns and in modern life because both thought and imagination are developed to a high degree of sophistication, but each separate from the other, namely thought as mere intellect, along with egotistic will, and imagination as images and pictures, along with industry, force and effort.

Profound suffering, true compassion and real happiness are therefore not modern and have not been modern for two millennia. However this does not mean that we cannot disabuse ourselves of our modernity as we come to grips with some of our contemporary necessities and needs.

*

3. Thought and imagination, as one, allow us also to contemplate suffering as an *outlook* – and more specifically as an outlook on *existence, survival* and *life*. The implication here is that it is not an outlook in terms of time, space and causality, nor is it, in turn, an appraisal, critique or judgment of existence, survival and life.

3a. So suffering as an outlook on *existence* reveals existence to us as an option fraught with risks and dangers not readily comprehended by the one who exists, especially if he or she insists on existing. Perhaps we need to be reminded that to exist is not the same as to be. Sadly the distinction is not a modern one. We need at least to be ready to suffer before that distinction can even appeal to us. Also, of course, it is not until we are able to suffer that existence is revealed to us as what it

31

really means, namely an exposure to what goes on without rhyme or reason, in abeyance of the truth, in the absence of light and in no way real. Existence is not this but means an exposure to it, for a short or a long time.

Needless to say, I suppose, in the name of wholeness, healing and happiness, we prefer being to existence (and to insistence!). At the same time our heart goes out to those who inadvertently embrace existence, especially modern existence, without knowing what they are doing. We are touched by their tragedy. If we feel that existence is not really their lot, we have compassion for them and will do everything in our power to introduce them to being and perhaps to suffering too. Those who are born to exist do not need our help in this regard.

*

3b. As for suffering as an outlook on *survival*, this brings us into contact with our various limits and limitations, in a way that accentuates the benefits to be drawn from them. It becomes obvious to us that we cannot grow unless we grow against something, although not to resist it or to quarrel with it but merely to draw strength from it. So our survival in this sense occurs to us as a death-orientation inasmuch as death is overcome and is by definition not a finality of life but that which always and again reminds us of life as a precious gift that cannot be permanently lost or even temporarily mislaid.

So survival as a death orientation for those who live makes good sense because without it we might become contemptuous of life rather than becoming more capable of living as we mature and more eager that our life should be rich in thought and imagination.

For the dead, survival is a bone of contention and something that has to be done, because death is the alternative. That sounds absurd because it is.

*

3c. Lastly, suffering as an outlook on *life* is more momentary than lasting, since life is eternal and we need but give in to it, once all the preconditions are in place. Nonetheless we sometimes need to be reminded of the ongoing need to mature and be fruitful rather than resting on our laurels and then we suffer, as it were, a resurgence of life which may, only temporarily, cast doubt on our very being. However once we have suffered a sufficiency, in perfectly sane expectation of renewal, the perception of eternal life is returned to us and we thrive with renewed vigour.

* * * * *

Ontology

To the extent that we are, rather than merely existing, merely translating appearances into experiences, we will very likely wish to be of some use to those who are not yet but bide their time in the mistaken perception of being as a non-committal, inauthentic and irresponsible opportunity.

Also to the extent that we are, we will take care of our environment, including all that pertains to us in terms of quality and worth, rather than following the various urges, drives, motivations etc. of our individuality at the expense of any thing or being at all.

Being therefore implies at least a degree of personal dedication to the good, while prior to such dedication we cannot possibly make any worthwhile judgment of the being of this or that, or, for that matter, of beings other than ourselves. Our own being is the priority for the legitimacy of whatever or whoever else we suppose might be.

*

To begin with, I am that I am and you are that you are. If no such beginning were available, how is it possible that we can recall a time when we no longer were as we wished or hoped we were? There must have been such a beginning, else all our dissatisfactions and disappointments with ourself would be moonshine and we might as well put our heads down and sleep.

Alas, we have no rest. We have nowhere to lay our heads. Something has happened to us that has disturbed our rest, otherwise how could we compare how we are, and whence the term rest? Is being then merely a wishful state, born out of disenchantment with – out of disillusionment with – whatever? Or shall we cast our lot in with those whose failing intelligence and imagination prevent them from becoming other than things that vacillate and debilitate?

*

We require no license to be. Nor do we need permission from any divine being before we enter upon our human being. And indeed it is our human being that interests us most passionately, since diminishment or even loss of it leaves us unidentified and disqualified in a crowd of nonentities that lingers near every point of the circumference within which we are that we are.

Being that we are, we are not merely human but human beings. No task is so crucial as the one that persuades us, now and for all time, of our human being. Nor do we care to acquaint ourselves with any discussion or explanation of being by anyone other than a human being, because only human beings, on account of their privileged position in the hierarchy of beings, are qualified for even commenting on being, whether in the particular or in general.

*

I cannot imagine myself not being, and yet I might not be. How is that to be understood?

In order to be a human being, constant attentiveness is required; we might remind ourselves of a time when due to activity of a certain vehemence we found ourselves staring into a veritable hole of non-being and knew fine well that we had once again overdone it and had neglected that nourishment, that accompanies what we do when we do it well. So doing had extracted itself from the human being and left – non-being. This is easy to imagine too, because after all we are not machines.

Then again we were, leisurely, in the fullest reflection of our presence here and now, a little dreamy to begin with per-

35

haps, then apparently losing ourselves pleasantly within ourselves, when suddenly an unpleasantness shook us out of what had become a state. A state had – become; and we? We no longer became and forfeited our wellbeing.

Over time we catch on that wellbeing is both being and becoming, however in such a way that we become conscious of this only if we – so to speak – mistake our cue. In other words, the duality of being and becoming is not real and only shows up if we lose ourselves in thoughtless being or in inordinate doing. Nonetheless it is worthwhile to keep this duality in mind, for the occasion when we go off the rails. Then we might say to ourselves: Oh dear, I neglected to be! Or, on the other side: Now I must become again, or else sink further into a mood for which we cannot be responsible.

So not being, strictly speaking, but <u>wellbeing</u>, offers us ontological riches, of which we may avail ourselves. We are not idle analysts nor busy synthesists.

When I say: I am that I am, I am in fact mindful of being and becoming as one. We should never imagine that we can be without doing or do without being, without at least an awareness of ourselves as doers. Since our perfection implies human being, we would always wish to remain substantial, which is to say human, in our case.

*

Any ontological effort, any undertaking to know and understand being, could also be seen as an attempt to assure ourselves of our soul and perhaps to come more thoroughly into the possession of it. Since our soul regularly manifests itself as our body and our mind, so that these two can be seen as right and left hand of our active and passive being during the operation of our dynamic or static soul, we cannot but conclude that any degree or amount of being, or wellbeing now, may also be viewed in connection with thought and equally on the basis of feeling.

What counts for us, meanwhile, is that we do not allow our study of, our enquiry into, being to detract from our own personal wellbeing. How readily this occurs we may observe both in ourselves and also in the work of certain so-called ontologists. So unless we retain our equilibrium, we will spend more time and effort seeking to re-establish it after repeated nervous lapses and vain supererogation than on patient knowing and understanding of what we mean by wellbeing and what it amounts to in reality.

Soul as body and mind, as thought and feeling. Not only "I think, therefore I am" but also 'I feel, therefore I am'. Not the soul, as an idea, but our soul, my soul, as ongoing operation and operations. Thoughtful being and felt being. Being as lively expression and colourful manifestation of our soul. The rejection of any attempt to turn our soul into a thing, or into a thing in itself. My soul as such makes no sense on heedless holiday from myself and that goes for being too, as a consequence. However, as my soul it does make sense, so that therefore as I am, so I am meaningfully and significantly – i.e. sensibly.

Being as the common denominator of existence and life – . I exist, therefore I must be. I live, so that naturally I am. There is the impulse, the human natural impulse, to be and then there is also the temptation, the unnatural, perverse temptation, not to be, to cease from being. The reason for the temptation is to confirm us in our human natural impulse and motivation. Well, what else.

*

Wellbeing announces itself initially as dream; also as vision. Indeed our first notion of it may occur to us as a vision. We do not sense this or that but we are, as it were wrapped by,

37

and engrossed in, eternity. As dream, eternity enters into our consciousness and gives an account of itself. It touches us creatively. Both vision and dream will, on such occasions, arouse in us a creative response to eternity; to eternal time, let us say. On such occasions we are neither feeling nor thinking individuals but we are – and we are well. Our immediate wish may be to communicate this wellbeing. However we are only accustomed to feeling or thinking that we are, so as a consequence this experience of eternal time impresses itself upon us in away that does not allow us, not for a while, to say how we are and perhaps not even that we are. We are astonished, puzzled, in wonderment and certainly it does not occur to us that this was a case of quite ordinary, normal wellbeing that was presented, or rather shown, to us. We compare it, after all, to how we have been all along, namely partial and not whole.

All depends now on whether or not we rise to the challenge. To put it bluntly, wellbeing is only for those who are willing to share. Being that is not wellbeing is never shared and lies idle in the psyche. There is absolutely no reason why anyone should take the least bit of interest in it. Wellbeing, by comparison, bypasses any psyche and attaches itself directly to the soul, stimulating it to creative action and passion.

I, whose soul is thus stimulated, and remarkably perhaps even stimulated in existence, will consider myself privileged or unpleasantly disturbed, depending quite literally on who I am. I may not get a second opportunity to be well. If I feel privileged, I will manage to overcome every reaction in myself, every nasty unwillingness to welcome this strange motivation and affection. There may be many such reactions. My willingness to overcome will be creative, and in this way, even in this way, I take advantage of the intimate creativity inherent in eternal time experienced (lived) by me as vision or dream.

*

"Hiding the pearl of great price."

When I am, do I yet live? If not, what else is required of me before I live?

If I am, do I have life?

Wellbeing is not a state but a word for how we are when we grow successfully. Any ontological findings therefore presuppose our awareness of ourselves as successfully growing human being. Obviously we cannot learn what being is; the attempt would be absurd. However, while aware of ourselves as growing, we may arrive at certain conclusions of how our wellbeing may be enriched or impoverished, and this is no small matter because, as was mentioned earlier, we would rather not forget or ignore that we are, and the richer our wellbeing, the less likely our indifference to it and the greater its prevalence in our thought and feeling.

What I refer to as an ontological finding pertains strictly to myself as a natural or born individuality. Such findings are unique to me and of peculiar value, therefore, to my community. Such findings may also be classified in accordance with their type. They may be typified. So, for example, it might occur to me to broaden my outlook in terms of certain ethical parameters to which I have become accustomed. Again, work would be involved and of course communication, so that a straight line of development would be established between my human nature and the members of my community, bringing us closer in a meaningful way.

*

We speak of wellbeing, to differentiate it from mere being, from merely being around, for someone absentmindedly or otherwise to point at, and not presenting something with integrity and stature, such as we mean by a being, in comparison, withal, to a thing. Oh that it might not be required to have

39

wellbeing and mere being before us and that only the one wonderful presence should ever meet our eye, however we live in a world where both the excellent entity and the shamefaced copy seek our appreciation on the stage of our environment and it behoves us to act accordingly.

Once we have acquired the mental habit of relating being, as wellbeing, to growth, namely to growth towards and during maturity, we should no longer hesitate to speak of that which is, being well, as a being, though we take out insurance against forgetfulness by setting beside and certainly slightly below our honourable being that which only pretends to be or can no longer, for various discernible reasons, afford to be, namely the thing.

Much as we would like, here too, to reacquaint ourselves with this most interesting half- or one quarter-being of things, we will discipline our discussion within the realm of being and beings, leaving mere being and things to one side.

Our purpose, as I touched on earlier, is the search for those ontological findings, that really have nothing to do, nor does our search have anything to do, with mere being and things, with how they come about or how they might be rescued and re-established, even resurrected. Let ontology be a discipline in its own right, untroubled by moral or even ethical considerations. Let us learn to revere beings and to honour them, for in that direction lies increased richness of life.

Often enough elsewhere I have drawn attention to the fact that humanity is the essence of being, of wellbeing, so that neither our human nature nor our creativity shall be kept to one side while we seek to establish beings in their rightful position within the terrain of our awareness. No more can I fly if I have no wings than I can set out on the path towards the wealth of being if my humanity is perverted or my human nature is overwhelmed by feelings of vanity and thoughts of might and greed. In other words, we must be proper human beings, unperturbed by popularity, before we can perceive real beings in their true light.

However, then nothing shall hold us back.

*

Now when I say unperturbed, I am right away and sensibly reminded how I should instead say: During such times as when we are unperturbed by popularity, and only during such times, can we have insight into the heart of beings and indeed we work both to guard against such perturbation and to liberate our spirit whenever it should have become affected, which happens, alas, both from the left and from the right, from above and from below – to keep us on our toes; what else.

Meanwhile our diligence in persevering with ontological pursuits allows us to grow ever more securely into our position as worthy human beings, ever more capable of transforming the popular threat into steadfast and manifold humanity. Why, the very knack we develop for strengthening our human being and rendering it habitual by and by, becomes customary and usual for us. The fact that we know that we are, becomes unshakeable, more and more, and our joyful knowledge that, whatever else happens, sudden inexplicable cessations of leisurely comfort and pleasant ease drawn into consideration, our being is such that it implies becoming, stays with us longer and saves us from childish despair more frequently.

Notwithstanding some traditional leanings, perhaps more often than not of a prejudicial character, we soon sense in ourselves a readiness to suggest that: We are, therefore we think, plus the logically coincident: We are, therefore we feel. Furthermore, since the 'therefore' strikes us as somewhat unfitting on account of that hint of causality, we might prefer: I am, thus I think and feel.

41

This thinking and feeling, equally exposed to the popular trivialization and determined for many centuries, in the west, in line with modern apprehensiveness in the face of final judgment, should be introduced from the beginning as well-thinking and well-feeling, akin to wellbeing. Unless we do not feel well, we do not feel truly and unless we think well, how can we be said to think really? And yet there will come a time, after sufficient ontology, when we can barely think and feel otherwise. Our body and mind will become so accustomed to keeping faith with our soul – our thinking will no longer hanker after divorced spirit, while our feeling will no longer betray our human nature – that in the absence of appreciable hindrance, we will cheerfully work towards endless world.

*

I am, thus I think and feel.

So what about these ontological findings, how do we go about those? Do we concern ourselves with thoughts and feelings?

Not a bit of it. Neither does my being, my wellbeing, depend on my thinking and feeling. What does it depend on then?

Are we not born into this world to be? Certainly we are. There is this kaleidoscope of our preferences and antipathies, right from the start, that should inform the unbiased onlooker of that singularity we demonstrate so soon after birth. We are individual human beings as soon as we start and if we were allowed and maybe given a bit of help and guidance we would go right on being individual human beings, each one of us here on the earth with some particular job to do. We are not told what it is, are we; we have to find out. Nothing could be simpler – if we lived on the moon. However we don't live on the moon, do we. We are right off introduced into diverse circumstances. There's this matter of the adults around us, for one thing. Then there's the climate, the geography and the geology – and the language. Oh my, yes, the language! Most impressive, right from that initial gurgle or wail – plus the reaction or the response to that. All calculated to inform and shape our being?

Chance would be a fine thing.

For our being – and I mean our human being now, our human wellbeing – to thrive, a whole lot of advantages and disadvantages have to come together, so that we have both something to go along with and something to struggle against. The will to be, for only one example, doesn't fall out of the sky. You may call it the will to be well. Nothing less really fills the bill. Oh yes, we can tell very early whether it is the will merely to be or to be well. Our intelligence first sharpens its knives on that. The gap between the two allows itself to be called a chasm and if a few parental adults knew about it, if they still remembered, they would come up with a little sympathetic intelligence and take a little pride in the process rather just in some dead end: 'Be good while Mummy is away!'

Be what? Be good? What does that mean, for goodness' sake?

It means do the best you can to deny that chasm. You may only be two years old, dear, but it's not too early to begin to live in denial. Your human nature dictates wellbeing; your environment, your circumstances, prefer mere being. Be good, do you hear!

'Was little Johnny good (for you) while I was away, Norma?'

'Oh yes. Not a peep out of him. He might as well be dead.'

'Oh, well, let's have a look, shall we? Perhaps he is.'

So there we have the chasm between mere being and well-being plus the intelligence that is getting to know it.

And then there's that notion of good being, and it's a curse.

*

I am certainly not the first to notice that gap, that chasm, between mere being and wellbeing but I may be the first to identify it as the source of passion and intelligent suffering.

Merely being, I open myself to interference (not influence) from the world of things, the finite world. Due to these contingent affects I become painfully aware of myself as self. I complain bitterly about my lot or strike out more or less viciously on a course of thoughtless, unfeeling behaviour. Merely being, I see no point in thinking or feeling – which does not prevent me from espousing the second-hand, namely thoughts and feelings. These I manipulate arbitrarily, wilfully or else I succumb to them, as to an overwhelming load of foreign material. Usually it is both of these in turns, though every individual leans more to one side than the other, again depending on circumstances. The individualist actually attempts to put all his money on just the one side, as victim or careerist.

We could go on forever, describing where mere being leads, but that would be pointless. Unsuffered pain is the hallmark, also intelligence that cannot come to grips with anything, properly. Left to itself, mere being leads straight to death, to death of person and soul. We are well enough acquainted with morality and religion in the service of mere being, with society at loggerheads with it and with the kind of this-worldliness that turns truth into falsehood, love into self-interest and hope into despair.

Enough said.

While mere being readily comes to hand because everywhere its manifestations stare us in the face, wellbeing has to

44

be learned and acquired. Our ontological enquiries, specifically, bring us into close range of the battleground, where mere being and wellbeing both appeal to us, for diverse reasons, but in terms of our soul and in reference to it. Satisfaction, a sense of wholeness, of accomplishment, the wish to fit in with something we can trust that has our best interests at heart – all this can be loosely described as the search for a viable soul – or as the ontological quest, which is not necessarily at all the paid pastime of academic philosophers.

*

The ontological quest – learning to differentiate between mere being and wellbeing and always again opting for the latter – .

Certainly wellbeing will gradually appeal to us as what we truly wish. Wishing and wellbeing can no longer be separated. We will draw faith into the process, because after the back and forth of not being able to make up our mind to the point where we behave and act accordingly, we find that it helps us to believe, that wellbeing is of the essence of our developing human nature. Our nature develops from the day we are born and this development will not make sense to us until we truly believe that wellbeing is to be intelligently preferred over mere being.

So we see now how a person who says 'I am' may mean something fundamentally different from an individual or an individualist who says 'I am'. Not that being differs from one person to the next but that one means wellbeing and the other mere being.

Of course the experience of wellbeing, once we know what it means in reality to be well, helps to set us more firmly on our course, but also opens us to a myriad mistakes and misunderstandings, and these in turn may be beneficially understood by us as encouragements to evolve, to be well in a myriad

45

ways. Development and evolution now proceed side by side, as our wellbeing becomes more intentional and more manifold. The intention to be well and the readiness to be well in different ways go on at one and the same time then. Our human nature does not stop developing once it begins to evolve.

*

To be well – in a myriad ways – what do we mean by that? The introduction of wellbeing into our lives is liable to condemn us to a period of indecision. For a time, very likely, we judged what all we depended on to be well, such as the right kind of food, just the right amount of stress in our daily lives, the love and affection of those around us and who knows what else. Every culture, every society, either dictates or persuades what is necessary to produce wellbeing. At times, wellbeing is also called happiness, satisfaction, contentment and so on, and for each of these a more or less credible or laudable recipe will have been worked out, by those who are the leading lights in the ancient or modern world. Wellbeing, in other words, is what people wish to achieve, to buy, to earn.

What we are saying here, however, is that we, as human beings, develop and evolve human naturally in terms of wellbeing and that if nothing interferes with our human natural development and evolution, we are well.

What we need to define therefore is not wellbeing but everything and all things that interfere with our evolution, such as confused ideals, harsh dogma, injustice and falsehood, unkind or cruel treatment and so on. Not those we hear about but those we personally experience should interest us; those we know in the flesh. Should we identify them, all the better to rid ourselves of them? Not at all. In the interest of our growth as human natural development and evolution, all these experienced hindrances and obstacles, whether pleasant or unpleasant, need to be discerned and recognized by us so that we may involve

46

them in our progress. Involution is a good word for what goes on while we ado not resist evil – and evil is the all-embracing concept for all that appears to go against us – but we discern the evil thing, or that which we experience as evil, for the sake of our growth. It helps us to overcome our fear of evil things and acts, once we learn how to involve them in our being.

*

Again, what do we mean by being well in a myriad ways?

What is it about our human nature that is essentially and effectively well? We know we do not grow in a vacuum. Whatever happens to us is a potential aid to our growth; we involve it. You might even say it involutes, each identified hindrance. However it does so because of our intelligent suffering of it and not if we ignore it or mistake it for unhappiness and misfortune against which we are powerless – or, and this has to be added – if we strive against it, if we fight it, if we hate it.

So this intelligent suffering is up to us. Also up to us is the wish to be well, as we mentioned earlier – and the wish to be well in a variety of ways.

Now consider the following: What is the point of our wishing to be well if our human nature is essentially well in any case? Is our wishing not a waste of time?

What we need to remember here is that we are not angels. We are creative and we work. There is our particular human nature and there is our participation in human/divine spirit. The two together account for our works. When we know ourselves as individual persons, we have one foot in each, one in nature and one in spirit. One hand builds and the other blesses.

So in view of ourselves as creative beings, the following word of the master applies: He who asks and knows that he has what he asks will surely receive it. We have it naturally,

47

we ask for it personally and then we have it as creative human being – as creating human beings.

Our human nature is not, after all, something that is readily accessible to our personal intelligence. We grow and we work, and it is possible for the two to become quite disparate, if we lose track of what we know and understand, of what we have learned and of what we remember. Not for nothing do we have a master, to whom we look for guidance and repair, for leadership and healing.

*

So after we wish that we were (well) and we have discovered our human nature and realized (believed) that it is essentially well, we might well wonder what else there is to be had. The knowledge of our well human nature is a precious secret. We make no display or exhibition of it. We do not advertise and publicize the fact that we know and are certain of the fact that insofar as we are, we are well, and that our wellbeing cannot be achieved, earned or bought but it is our human nature. Of course we cannot help but let it shine through that we are well and that our wellbeing is our essential human nature, however eventually the time comes for us not only to be well but to do well.

Once again, this doing well is not performed, in accordance with some external standards or on the basis of extinct tradition but in line with the spirit of truth is it done, and to incorporate the spirit that is truth.

In addition to this, our doing is done in terms of world without end and little by little these terms are more and more experienced by us, so that we may be well at home in our world and our fellow human beings may have the advantage and use of our works, as we have the benefit of theirs.

Quickly the new day dawns.
The first birds are active,
They venture out in the early light.
Gulls hurry about, as if to
Put the final touches on the night.

Now a vermillion brushstroke
Attracts our gaze in the eastern sky,
Where soon the master of the day
Will roar into splendid view
To destroy every vestige of darkness.

*

The wish to do well becomes strong in us. Again, we may refer to it as simply the wish to do, however there is this opportunity merely to do. There merely is that opportunity. Can we tell the difference? If we just want to get it done, there can be no creativity. What we do well is endless. Timeless and endless.

It stands to reason that we cannot continue to be well once we begin merely to do. Our being does not cease once we begin to do. So what we merely do also forces us to merely be and how little time it might take before we notice how vilely we harm ourselves!

Our mere being, in other words, is liable to affect our thinking and feeling, our sensing and conceiving, first and foremost in the way that the two will no longer be one. Our doing and behaving, while we merely are, is disjointed, erratic and self-destructive, so who would for long elect to put up with that!

The time has come to return to our known being, for we wish to be well and we know that in truth our human nature bears within it no such separation as we have suddenly taken note of within us. Ontologically there is no reason why we shall not, post haste, return to our precious wellbeing. A moment's reflection might do the trick. We may have to stand back and reorient ourselves. We may have to leave entirely whatever it is we are in the train or strain of doing and return to our more or less metaphoric little chamber. I say 'more or less' advisedly.

There may come a time when we are bereft of doing, when we do not wish to do any particular thing but we interpret this as a set-back. There is the urge to do and we cannot think or imagine what to do.

This very likely comes down to our having become addicted, more or less, to being active. We suppose our goal must lie in mere activity. It happens readily. I enjoy my work, we say. I love my work. And then: I have to work, I cannot stop.

Then, mercifully, the cessation of work is imposed upon us and as our intelligence once again comes alive after having been swamped by mere business, we may gratefully acknowledge we have experienced mercy.

Our awareness of merciful spirit is crucial. We may be assured that even our wellbeing partakes of mercy and what a pleasure it is to know that! Those who are christian will say that the father pleases us presently. We wish to be well and we know that we are well. We desire to be merciful and we imagine our human nature is fundamentally merciful.

Desire and imagination have come together here and we do not regret it. Again, there is such a thing as mere desire and mere imagination. Right from the beginning, when we wish to be well and then we know we are well, and we begin to take wellbeing for granted, we wish also to do well, for it satisfies us immensely. Then we experience mercy, for mercy limits us and we know that the spirit of mercy stops us from going too far in one direction or the other. We have learned that this is so. Perhaps someone has told us and we have had the grace to accept what we were told, so that now we can literally afford, ontologically speaking, to imagine and to desire, for we will be more likely to do so well rather than merely.

And always and again we remain perfectly at liberty to indulge in mere desire, in mere imagination. What is our goal? What is our purpose? That is what we need to ask. For if desire and imagination are not merciful – are not informed by merciful spirit, by the father spirit – they would lead us astray and we, by doing so, would lead others astray – if the spirit of mercy did not call a halt in time. We may be assured that it does – unless, of course, we are not well to begin with – in which case we may find ourselves assailed by creative spirit.

*

Those who get caught up in mere being, are invariably fascinated by language, and speech, and talk, not to mention babble. This is not surprising, because the very language we speak reflects our true being and as a consequence our interrogation of language itself cannot but interrupt and undermine our wellbeing. If we have nothing to say, we should keep quiet until we have something to say, rather than inverting and perverting our faculty of communication. What about an analysis of signs? I can imagine myself desiring such a thing on any occasion when I am unkindly pressured to come up with something when I have nothing on hand. It would amount to a defence mechanism. If not that, then surely an illness.

*

So what does it mean, what are we to make of it, when someone says: I am glad, or: I am sad? It depends entirely on who he is. Is his being wellbeing or it mere being. We can tell, can't we, by listening to him. Of course we have to listen well and not merely. Whatever anyone says who merely is, cannot

51

possibly make much difference to us because we have no way of reaching him or her. All we hear is: I merely am. If in addition to this we hear: I merely am but I wish I were well, then we can do something, however never directly in line with, or in response to, any expressed particularity, because this would only confirm that beleaguered individual in mere being – in his or her mere being. Nothing can help except what we say from our own wellbeing. Often it suffices for us simply to express our sorrow in the presence of someone who is caught up in mere being, even while avoiding any direct reference to what has been said to us. Should mere being turn into ill-being, we are bound to feel we are being forced, in which case especial care is needed not to confirm the stricken individual in his illness – by attempting to argue him out of some position he seems to hold or by visibly falling in with it. Ill-being is damage at the root and not to be scoffed at.

We are liable to get side-tracked here and forget that our pursuit is ontological.

'Are you well?' Yes, thank you for asking. I was a bit under the weather yesterday but I'm fine today.

'Oh dear! I didn't realize, when I spoke to you yesterday, that you were unwell.'

This is obviously not what we mean by wellbeing and mere being. Ontological wellbeing is nothing more than a way of saying that it is possible to be without really being. Our recognition of mere being, and our reference to it, is not a matter of academic trifling either. Our purpose is to acquaint ourself with the fact that first and foremost we ourselves, but of course also others, might fall into, slide into, get caught up in, a way of being that is unsubstantial, inhuman, impersonal, soulless. We do not even have to do wrong; we can be wrong. Even prior to making a nuisance of myself, I might be ineffectual and superficial. Add to this, that being nothing is more serious than doing nothing and that alone by being we influence, for good or ill, and little by little a genuinely ontological pursuit, like our own here, is bound to occur to the doubtful onlooker as not at all a worthless pastime.

Quite by the way, we should not suppose that the much quoted Cartesian utterance: Cogito, ergo sum, (I think, therefore I am) was intended as an ontological statement. Otherwise one might as well respond with: I am, no wonder I think. Or: I think; I wonder if I am. And so on, to amuse the idle.

*

Finally what counts is that being is such that I can wrongly suppose that I am and that I am responsibly accountable even for my being. As I pass from morality to ethics, I learn that all those 'thou-shalt-nots' refer exclusively to my doing and that the time has come for me to realize that even being desirous of another woman in my heart is adulterous; that even being imaginative in the service of extinct knowledge is adulterous; that even language in the use of self-justification and self-assertion is adulterous. Not for nothing did we observe that not between being and non-being, which is a vain comparison and an entirely misleading contrast, but between wellbeing and mere being, a yawning indifference is liable to open and a contemptible abyss may inform us of our impotence, of our hopelessness and lack – even shortfall – of human natural affection. And the last is the greatest that threatens. In he face of the call, the need, the demand for human natural affection, we may stand convicted of the most serious failing and defect for which we may beheld accountable and responsible.

For we grow and our growth is liable to be abrupt. We cannot expect, we cannot foretell the time of our next growth stimulus, for it must occur when we least expect it, ("when we are not looking"), otherwise, in our comparative ignorance, we would surely strive to protect and defend ourselves against it,

53

so desirous do we become of the status quo; so eagerly do we imagine the endless continuation of what we know so far. Are we prepared for the shock that will stun us, for we have no language to say it?

Needlessly dramatic language.

That which gives us the next push forward as we grow in reality and the merciful spirit – neither is nor merely is. Neither does it automatically fall in with our wellbeing nor can we recognize it as mere being. What does this mean? We do well to be watchful, to be prepared, in our daily existence, "for the son of man comes when we least expect him".

This growth-principle – how careful we need to be in the handling of it! Only the dead do not grow, and when they die we look the other way.

Practically, our readiness is a case of delegation of mere being or wellbeing. There is a great deal that seems, at first, to stimulate our growth, however upon reference to our doctrine, to what we have learned so far in our lives, we will assign it to mere being and it is of no further interest to us. If, on the other hand, it really is and truly pertains to our wellbeing, nothing further is required of us, for we have even now recommenced to grow.

*

Not only is it our task to warn of the arrival of the one who is neither wellbeing nor mere being but equally is it up to us to identify him in terms of wellbeing once he has arrived – and to cast aside all that would have him in terms of mere being. I say it is our task, however, not only in line with this ontology, the ups and downs of which we characterize by means of our thought processes, steeped in being, but also as human beings do we make it our business to enlighten one another with regard to the one who is, who actually is among us, and only as

54

we distance ourselves from him, and to the extent that we do, must he 'return' in that sense, perhaps to be entirely misunderstood as misfortune or at least partly recognized as the one from whom we have our being, our wellbeing.

So we have our being in gratitude from the one who is. Alas, that it should be our ongoing business to spend such gratitude and to know him among us who is wellbeing entirely inasmuch as we know him correctly and love him intimately. From him we have our wellbeing when our human natural affection for one another is alive and thriving. Among us then he aids and abets our human natural affection. Then we behave like fools and he turns into the one who was and will be, phenomena both of a nature that shares in both wellbeing and mere being, while we await the time of his unexpected arrival, which may well surprise, stun or even shock, for we cannot be perfectly ready, since we can do nothing perfectly in his not-being, as it is bound to appear to us.

Let each and every human being see to his or her own wellbeing in the light of how reality is experienced. Certainly we can be of help to one another. On the basis of what has been seen and told here, there cannot possibly be any argument over correct interpretation, fitting credentials or such like. Can we not see it in one another's eyes where the shoe pinches? Only human natural affection can sweep away the clouds to reveal the polestar – can cleanse the source of our being so that wellbeing may gush forth while mere being loses face.

* * * * *

Reading
(remedial)

From the novel: It's Everyone for Himself
(or Herself)

Reading is generally thought of as an activity in its own right and possibly in a different league from ordinary experience and therefore to be approached in other ways. When children go to school they learn to read but under very specific circumstances which vary a great deal depending on what sort of a person the teacher is, on the cultural environment of the children and of course on what is generally expected in that particular school curriculum and school room.

When we try to imagine what is required for ordinary experience, of the natural world, for example, we can readily come up in ourselves with such faculties as knowing, understanding and imagining. Perhaps these three are even the principal components of our experience, although of course as usual, the whole is greater than the sum of the parts. Memory probably plays an important role and any previously acquired experience, such as a body of knowledge. We can keep dividing and splitting up all these faculties into a never-ending number of components and we still won't come closer to the actual experience, which requires the doing of it, in the present case the actual reading, because as soon as we talk or think 'about' something we are not actually doing it, so that initiative, good will, pleasure, hope of reward and fear of punishment, to name but a few, do not play the same role. Theory and practice only overlap during creativity and creation.

Personally I can see no real reason why reading should not be approached in the same way as ordinary world experience. In that case *knowledge, understanding and imagination* would count as much here as elsewhere. When we mention knowledge we include insight, memory, perception, cognition, cerebration and so on. Understanding, in its turn, involves love, fantasy, mercy, humility, while imagination might include picture, symbol, myth, legend, mystery etc.

Now the two main components of every human being are **body** and **mind**, feeling and thought, and if either of these are undernourished or not given free play, all experience, including the reading of language, suffers.

So we both think and feel when we properly know, understand and imagine. There is something to be said for simplicity. Body and mind, sense and concept, work together, in tandem or as one, in a mature human being. We aim for this as we grow up and grow older. We wish not just to be adults, over the age of eighteen or whatever the law dictates, but mature adults and this means that we wish to develop both our mind and our body, both our sense apparatus and our technique for forming concepts.

I can think of no reason to leave anything of this out when we bring children up. All of it plays into every skill we teach, or rather show, our children and that includes reading. Reading and writing of course go together in an important sense. My point is that when we show children how to read and write, we should go about this in the same way as when we show them how to dress themselves, how to behave in the presence of friends and strangers, how to help with cleaning the house and cooking meals, how to play honourably and respectfully with other children and so on.

In all these cases, our central aim has to be the parenting of the child. In other words, how we bring a child up depends on how we teach all these things. Our main aim when we teach a child how to peel potatoes is primarily to bring that child up and only secondarily that he or she should help with the preparations of a meal. A more insightful notion of what is involved in parenting will allow us to do a better job when we help children with specific talents and skills.

We often observe how superficially the same theory in teaching is applied by two adults or by two schools or two remedial programs and one succeeds remarkably better than the other and this is not because the more successful one was more faithful to the theory but because the principle ambition was upbringing and the particular skill was allowed to remain in a secondary position, in terms of the 'parental' approach.

For the purpose of this essay I use the term 'parental' to denote all that adults, hopefully more mature adults, do to benefit children. Fathers, mothers, aunts and uncles and grandparents, teachers, friends can all benefit children 'parentally' by helping them to achieve their potential, eventually, as maturing adults.

Also, by the way, teaching is not the same as education. I take teaching to mean any parental introduction to a child of new experience and skills, By education I mean something else, namely the liberation of anyone, child or adult, from both incurred and inherited misfortune. If I may use some specialist vocabulary to make my point, anyone who wants to help a child overcome such hindrances as dyslexia or hyper-lexia, which presumably are largely hindrances to reading, is undertaking to educate that child. Any educational effort is therefore in an important sense remedial and corrective, which is to say liberating.

I am going to limit myself in this essay to the discussion and exploration of parental education in terms of reading. I am going to leave to one side parental teaching, of language skills or suchlike.

It stands to reason that if we wish to remedy and correct, we must surely have in mind some right and proper and pos-

58

sibly even good way of being or doing, of acting and behaving. So unless we know, understand and imagine what it means to read and how an experience of reading can be satisfactory and rewarding, we cannot help anyone overcome mistaken notions, faulty practices and unfortunate approaches and attitudes with respect to reading.

One more point: Allowances have to be made for humanity. Where human beings are concerned, of whatever age or imperfection, the main driving force, the central urge for excellence, the essential purpose of being and becoming, is humanity. So how do we make room and space for humanity? By loving. While we do not love, we do not educate. If we cannot love we cannot educate. If we will not love, all our educational efforts are bound to fail, in the short or in the long run.

So this appears to be a weighty task. *Love* is of the essence. Our body and our mind are to be at full alert. We would function in terms of knowledge, understanding and imagination. Now we are ready to help another human being. We will not merely be tinkering with a few side issues and raise hopes shortly to be dashed. We will not be merely manipulating someone's trust so that our sense of self will be aggrandized. We will not flatter ourselves that we are doing good when in fact we give birth to some slap-dash theory with which we tantalize and terrorize our unfortunate fellow men, women and children.

*

The main issue with reading is language. We learn to babble, to talk and some of us even learn to speak – almost without giving it another thought. The quality of it depends mostly on the company we keep. Not entirely but mostly. How do we measure this quality? Again by the degree to which it aids and abets human growth.

Exactly the same goes for the quality of writing. The effort I make to read is the same as the effort I make to listen to someone talking or speaking. Written text is nothing more than a record of babbled, talked or spoken language. If nothing but babble is written, I don't care whether I can read or not. I am ignoring the transfer of bits of information now, which is not unimportant. Tesco sells the cheapest oranges. Turn left at the intersection. Please send flowers to 29 James Street. That sort of thing. It's nice if we can read that, but I know a sixty-year old man who is skilled and has managed very well indeed in our highly civilized society, although until now he could not write or read at all. He is a mature man right enough but there is also something cheerfully childlike about him, unspoiled. It makes me wonder.

In the absence of love, nothing can be properly learned. I mentioned that and I truly believe it. Now what about the sense aspect. I can see the written word in front of me and I can also see the visual representation of that word in my mind. My body and my mind are a married couple. Each one fills in where the other has left a gap. I also get a feel for words. There is the image, the picture and the feel of the word. Whoosh, the stooping falcon. Splash, the trout back into the lake. Rat tat tat, the machine gun. Who can hear the cut in slice, in knife; the popping of the cork; the spit, sparking, sparkle of the fire; the crushing of the grapes. We see those words and it is as if we heard, as if we felt what is going on. We read them and its as if someone were saying them. Written language represents. We can literally – using letters – evoke, provoke. All this is bodily.

We connect words up in phrases and sentences and our mind comes into play. Even phrases, like 'the tension of the violin string' or 'into the tall grass' have mental potential. I begin to put two and two together. Sentences carry a burden of conceptual meaning for us. 'Let me help you through that crisis'. 'There is too much sugar in my tea.' 'The sky is blue.' Simple statements, a complaint, an offer of help – mind and body are working together, because feeling and emotion may be traced in situations and under conditions. We may even bare our soul, without the distinct aid of body or mind: 'A thousand fears explain to me / how much I loved you while you lived.'

Now for *knowledge*, understanding and imagination: How much do we have to know in order to read? We have to know a few letters and how they come together to give rise to words. It helps to know about vowels and consonants but some people only take mental pictures of words and learn them that way. It helps to know the difference between the names of letters and the sounds they are liable to make. Most languages include silent letters and letter groups in their written words. Many words in English, for example, are written the same way but do not mean the same and are pronounced differently. Content and content: The content of that play leaves me content. Read and read: I can no longer read what I read yesterday. Some are spelled the same and sound the same but have different meanings: 'Wait a second, it's the second one I want.' Some are pronounced the same but both mean something different and are not spelled alike. From 'here' you can 'hear' the waterfall. Not and knot; pore and pour; sleigh and slay. At a distance of ten feet, all three of the following, if spoken casually, sound the same: paradise, parrot eyes, pair of dice.

Do we need to know all this? Do we need to know about prefixes and suffixes, about verbs and nouns, present and past and future tense? Dative and genitive? Not at all. We don't need it for speaking and we don't need it for reading. However if we want to make ourselves understood, knowledge can give us a boost. Orthography, which is conventionally correct spelling and phrase and sentence formation is helpful knowledge. We pick much of this up from people around us but we can take a look at it and take an interest in it.

We *know* 'how' to read but we *understand* 'what' we read. We may be able to read without understanding but what is that worth? All too often children are taught how to read while their understanding is totally ignored. The understanding involves us in what we read. We become part of the text and it becomes part of us. Conception, perception lets us take hold of what we know and make something out of it, change it, overcome it and so on. In the absence of understanding we stumble through life as if we were blindfolded; we make no progress, neither within nor without. Should we be asked to learn how to read text that requires neither conception nor perception? Should such text exist in the first place?

Well, it does. So eventually we do well to learn how to read critically. In that case we consciously separate the corn from the chaff. Of course we may also read perceptively, and then all we do is look for the quality and the value, like children, and if we see none we pass on to something else, without making judgments.

However, whether we read perceptively or only critically, first we have to learn how to read. Our judgment can be developed quite separately. A man can know quality from junk without ever learning how to read? If he knows this, he will reject junk once he has learned how to read. Meanwhile let us begin by teaching children how to read quality texts.

When it comes to that, should anything at all ever be done in sloppy fashion? And yet, look at what schoolchildren are asked to peruse? They are bound to be bored if they have any intelligence at all to start with. How can they pay attention to what bores them? Sooner rather than later they are diagnosed as suffering from attention deficit syndrome. What happens to their hungry human nature, to their appetite for concrete spiritual nourishment, in an environment where the fare is grit and chaff?

I have watched these children when, under the duress of the teacher's disapproving manner, they are constrained to 'decipher'. There is no content at all in what they are being asked to read. What a shame!

Imagination is a blessing. It allows us to play with the world and the world doesn't mind.

Imagination oils our body and greases our mind. I put it like that because in the absence of imagination our body and mind tend to become mechanical.

Not all are equally endowed with this faculty but surely, prior to abuse, everybody can imagine a little! We can encourage one another to trust and to learn to trust, sufficiently for imagination to develop again. Imagine a society where all people are magnanimous! Imagine a purple cloth hanging from the sky. Imagine you can read. Imagine two or three written words.

Picturing is, or course, not the same as imagining, but it's a start. Mental pictures of written letters and words can be helpful. Some of us, some children too, have lost even that ability. What we don't use we lose – a conventional wisdom. So, how can we expect to retain, not to mention improve, our powers of imagination if we observe virtual appearances for hours every day? Radio at least still energized the habit of picturing but it made so much of it that even in that case, where picturing is a primary faculty, imagination fades into the background and when we call on it, – rarely, let's face it – nothing is there.

Well, watching television puts paid even to picturing. Now reading has at best turned into a mechanical skill. For years we have seen how special efforts were made in schools to 'intrain' this mechanical skill wherever so-called 'problem children' cropped up. What these programs said was: Remain a mechanical thing and learn mechanical reading. But very few children are content being treated mechanically. The more intelligent ones rebel.

All it takes is for a more imaginative group of educators to come in and these so-called 'problem children' perform well beyond those who do not yet present an actual problem. Of course they like the special attention too but surely anything that rescues children from a living death is worthwhile.

Now learn to read while imagining what it might say, considering the context too, of course. No one should be asked to read out of context. This is why imaginative teachers often start children off by asking them to read words they are familiar with. Words within the child's familiar context. *(see Sylvia Ashton Warner)*

A great many children's books are repetitious clap-trap. What a crime, to serve up to children what they will become addicted to and therefore continue to buy! Very well, the child is already bored and unable to imagine, so that child must be excited. My child, says Mrs. Jones proudly, reads at least four books a week. Really? What does he read? Here, The Witches in the Kitchen – Magical Terror Ghosts – Bad Boy Billy. I wonder, would it not be better if he read less? If a decent imaginative children's book came along, I mean quality writing and not claptrap, it wouldn't be able to hold its own, I mean financially, in the presence of all these wizards, ghosts, magicians, werewolves, bats out of hell. But that's fantasy! No it isn't. It's escapism.

We know how to read, we understand what we read and we imagine why what we read is like that and not different.

A boy walks up the middle of the street. (Why is he walking up the middle?) He suddenly runs down a side street and disappears into a broken-down old shed. (Why does he suddenly run? Why into a shed? Why is the shed broken down and old?)

Imagination asks all those questions. Quality text will supply the answers and the reading experience will be whole.

Who distinguishes quality text from clap-trap then, if children are not to be bothered with that judgment? Why, the parental adults in their vicinity of course. Surely they take the upbringing of their children seriously. Surely they will inform themselves of the difference between quality text and twaddle.

Alas.

If all else fails, and I fear that all else has failed in many places, hopefully caring adults with a degree of maturity and a little wisdom will make it their business to educate – a few, several, perhaps many children – so that at least some of their neglected faculties will be enlivened again and perhaps they will do it in terms of reading. Why not? Perhaps in terms of writing too. Or in terms of intelligent, imaginative playing. So much of that has gone to the wall, hasn't it.

*

Parental education in terms of reading and writing is not the same as the teaching of reading and writing. It might be wise to take a look at what it means to learn how to read and write in the first place, quite separately from some effort at remedy and correction if bad habits have been formed or if impediments of one sort or another, to conventional practice, exist.

Surely writing is not a whole world apart from the performance of an art. A child may experience quite a thrill when first carving his initials into a tree. A few years later he writes love-letters. Expression and communication are creative acts and, by way of creation, human beings discover their soul and then enlarge it. I have never come across a child who does not like to draw or to paint. We tend to associate art with what painters, composers and sculptors do, in other words with artists but artists are specialists in a type of creativity. What I mean by human creativity is more fundamental and we have no trouble observing it in children. Playing and pretending are likely to be seriously creative.

So here we are in the presence of a most fundamental human trait, which is creativity. Perhaps positive expression and communication sum it up. Writing and reading, together, arise out of this basic instinct for creating, against all odds, a personal world for ourselves and then enlarging it, enriching it, qualifying and justifying it. They arise out of it along with many other creative drives, urges and wishful activities.

Surely we will encourage children to read and write differently if we keep this creative need of theirs in mind, rather than assuming that we impose upon the child some behaviour to any degree foreign to his nature! No, most children are quite capable of taking pleasure in reading and writing, unless some other creative urge is very strong and therefore demanding prior attention. For example we hear of children who, in order to experience some satisfaction at all, will insist on learning to play some musical instrument, even from the age of two or three, so that reading and writing are not at all a priority. Usually however children are quite ready to approach reading and writing at a fairly early age, cheerfully and agreeably – unless they are introduced to it as though it were a chore, as something they must do or else, as a mechanical skill that has nothing to do with themselves as growing, human natural beings but only with external, 'extinct', dead matter and means. If the latter, it would be silly not to expect acts of rebellion, psychic hindrances, and *the surfacing of inherited misfortunes.*

As we return to our topic now, which is the parental liberation of children from hindrances to a casual development of reading and writing skills, we can see how we may be wise to proceed in the light of reading and writing as potential forms of creativity, which therefore reach right down into a child's dynamic human nature. We have a lot to keep in mind and we will be glad to do so because then our remedial and corrective intentions are bound to arise out of our own native desire for verifying and beautifying our communal world. We will not be mechanics but creators. What a world of difference!

*

Possibly it makes more sense that any remedial intention should proceed right from the start in terms of both reading and writing at once. Children, like adults, would like to be able to make sense of the marks they make on paper. They want to understand what those marks mean and they would like to be able to imagine what use they are. Surely writing should come first, if not actually coinciding with reading. I suppose any acquired ability merely to read would soon fade if it were not accompanied by writing. Of course we are all liable to both read and write absent-mindedly, superficially, hurriedly, with no attention paid to why we are doing it and as a consequence our imagination starves. This is why passive television watching, along with all other digestion of mass media, destroys our imagination. We could not possibly come up with a good reason why we are doing this. Remember that our imagination responds to the question 'why' and that it is due to active, engaged imagination that our body and mind are able to come to any organic agreement, so that they may marry and so that we may be whole, rather than fragmentary beings, things, without a centre.

*

How could we help to revive imagination in terms of reading and writing? There must be a million ways, depending on who wants to do it. However keeping in mind the nature of imagination, we might try the following:

Why is the word 'trap' written like that? Because it springs shut.

Why does sizzle have two zeds in it? It could be because of water in the hot fat. What do you think?

How would you spell spring? Why, imagine all those buds appearing suddenly on twigs and branches, those young lambs leaping in the wet grass!

How come 'book' has two o's in it? Because you 'look' into it with two eyes.

Of course we would begin with words the child uses himself every day. We are not training him to come first in spelling bees. We are enlivening his imagination. We, as instructors, have continually to use our own imagination, otherwise it turns into a mechanical exercise. Like trying to explain love without loving.

Why not ask the child why he thinks 'fork' is spelled like that? Why spoon has a big hollow in it? Why 'knife', 'gun', 'sky', 'dream' sound like that?

Guard against sentimental gushing. Curb the enthusiasm. Imagination is cool.

Imagination helps a child become familiar with a word before being asked to write or read it. This can be very important. Can you say 'cackle' without sounding like a hen? Can you say 'fire' without your brain lighting up? Why would you 'bleed', and not 'cough'? When you 'sprint', could you 'sprain' your ankle?

The really effective measure of remedial imaging occurs to us while we deal with a given child – in response to whatever arises at the moment. Don't we have faith in our <u>affective spontaneity</u>? Especially when we get annoyed at the child, for making that same mistake yet again, for looking bored, for acting stupid when we know he isn't – out of our loving overcoming of our annoyance will 'happen' totally new and perfectly appropriate measures for solving that particular annoying problem. It would be most worthwhile, if this way of solving problems could be taught to parental adults. You feel stumped, you take a deep breath, you wait a moment while you pay attention and suddenly you know what to do this time. This is much better than using the same method and it should at least always be kept ready along with any given method.

Our imagination delights in coming up against knotty problems. Such delight is infective and readily transferred. It will soon take the place of any acquired anxiety and so clear the path for more cheerful learning.

So many of the problems associated with reading and writing originate in anxiety. An anxious child is not in touch with his imagination. It's as if the school had no playground. Imagination is the playground of our mind. Children love to play with words, to turn them this way and that, to connect them in unusual and entertaining ways. This should be encouraged wherever anxiety lies at the root of any hindrances. What's the point of correct spelling, of neat handwriting, of proper phrases and sentences, it the child no longer has an imaginative bond with language? Let's always keep in mind that something has been damaged, perhaps even during a previous generation, and needs to be healed, something has been frightened off and needs to be trusted and retrieved. We usually underestimate how much damage neglect and merciless behaviour by adults can do to children of any age. Some children are not brought up at all but are allowed to drift towards adulthood, where they remain immature for the rest of their lives. Others are not brought up but forced up and have known little joy in their lives; not to mention actual child abuse, due to which the incurred harm is far-reaching.

In all these cases a remedial teacher can work wonders – even by limiting herself to helping the child in terms of reading and writing skills. Love too is far-reaching.

*

Let's take a look now at how a child understands language, read and written language especially.

I said earlier that cognition addresses the 'what' of our experience. What exactly is going on here? What does this teacher want from me? I would like to *understand* that. I have a notion as to why I would like to learn more words and I can imagine that reading and writing them can be a pleasure but what happens to me when I read a word or write a word? When I read or write entire sentences and paragraphs, perhaps even a story? What should I expect will happen?

That is one set of 'what' questions. They are a little more deep-seated and are often overlooked. A child, at least inwardly, will ask them all the same. We, the parental adults, will not enter upon a discussion with the child relating to these questions but our awareness of them is important for improving cognition. The question 'What does it mean?' lives and breathes within the aura of: 'What does it mean to me?' 'Does it mean anything at all to me? Will I be punished if I let what it means affect me?'

Here we come around to the thorny problem of how *understanding* is defeated rather than encouraged. Again, let's keep in mind that as soon as the child is born into the world he or she wants to understand. What's all this? I haven't seen this before and I demand an explanation. It touches me and I need the meaning of it.

The babe cries if this understanding is not forthcoming.

Nothing infuriates a toddler so much as when he knows what he wants but can't have it. What is the reason for my will? I want to understand this pressure in my chest, that makes it hard for me to continue to breathe normally. All I get is: Don't do this! Don't do that! – What's going on here?

Meaning makes our world interesting, bearable and palatable. We live and we want meaning. We don't get it and we turn inward, away from this world. Our existence, our behaviour, becomes problematic. We are never too young to 'have issues' with our world experience. Psychoses take hold of us. A child's mind is no longer properly accessible.

So how do we encourage understanding in a child, in terms of reading and writing?

Asking a child questions about what he has just read merely annoys him and makes him feel guilty. Maybe next time he will be careful and try to pre-empt any questions while he reads. I must remember what it says here – or else! Understanding inspired by fear of disapproval, of a low mark, can only be avoided if we can somehow bring the child back to the way he experienced his natural environment, observing it and engaging with it. What something means to me depends entirely on my experience of it, so far, under conditions as they have existed for me – so far. I will wish to understand if I can promise myself a reward for doing so. It should be a pleasure to understand the meaning of something. Consequently text has to be meaningful. A story has to have significant content. Perhaps my access to it has to be facilitated but there must be something of value there that will make my access worthwhile.

Surely at first whatever text a child is asked to read should draw its meaning from that child's own existence. Not only should the words be familiar to him but he should also be able care for, to care about, what goes on, for example if the text is a description of something. Also, if a diagnosis shows that the child is low on imagination, not too much imagination should be demanded from him at the start. That goes without saying. Let him find his way in line with his strengths. Then later we can gradually introduce him to whatever element or faculty he seems to be weak in or to lack. Faculties are imagination, intellect, intelligence, intuition and instinct. Commonly a child is strong in at least one or two of these. An educator will soon get to know where the shoe pinches.

We can understand in terms of all five of these. Or, we may observe that all five require a level of understanding in order to work, to operate, in the child's favour. The question: 'What exactly is going on here?' will then be answered imaginatively, intuitively, etc. 'What do you make of this particular word?' 'What do you suppose would go well with it?' 'What do a cat and a mouse have in common?'

Especially that last question might be answered in a great variety of revealing ways. I mean revealing for the educator. Again, in the educational companionship of the child, it will occur to him what to ask. We cannot possibly make up a stock of questions. He will notice how that child understands and he will reflect on why the child responded or perceived in one way or another. So much of this is down to the educator's experience. Knowledge and imagination play into our understanding.

* * * * *

The Body and the Blood of Jesus the Christ
(a fragment)

I approach this as someone who knows absolutely nothing about it and therefore open myself to the charge of dishonesty, but my curiosity is great and so is my willingness to learn. I wonder, am I proposing to look at something that is of no practical use whatsoever to contemporary living or do I promise myself a source of good power here by bringing up to date a notion that has had theologians labouring for Christian centuries. I can usually depend on it, that if something exists, it will sooner or later reveal its being to me while I keep an open mind and approach it more or less like a child, unprejudiced and with the innocence of a child. Not being a learned man, I find this easier than some. The difficulty resides in limiting myself to a few pages, so I intend to draw heavily on my thought as recorded in books I have written in the past.

What occurs to me at the outset is, that what I have valued most all my life is a single and unshakeable foundation for all my human faculties, my thinking and believing, my seeing and feeling, my speaking and behaving and so on. That I eventually came to think of this as a typically philosophic ambition is neither here nor there right now. The point is that human being desires to be truthful, which calls for a readiness to adopt and adjust to an ever changing reality on our part.

The clown in me seeks to overcome tragedy with laughter. The saint in me would like to be able to approach all unpleasantness with fortitude. The hero in me denies all unpleasantness and concentrates on strength. The Christian in me is glad of the opportunity to be able to approach divinity as an equal. The heathen in me insists on his primitive humanity as a source of strength. Are there others worth mentioning? The citizen in me has an interest in an orderly existence. The creator in me values nothing so much as his ability to transform pain into substance. The father in me is glad to be able to draw on the paternal qualities of merciful providence.

And so on and so on.

These are not roles I play but some aspects of my multi-layered personal human nature. They make for a wealth of liveable life. Where would I be, without that single, central foundation! I come back to it for everything I need. I go out from it to everywhere I want to go. What I do, rests on it and what I become, relies on it.

*

There was a time when I relied on this foundation without knowing. That was when I was a child. Later there was the time, (which is also now), when I was aware of this foundation and knew I could rely on it. I grew to this awareness, thanks to the mature parental adults who cared for me and also due to certain artworks I learned to draw into the process. Thirdly, and perhaps most importantly, I rely on this foundation on account of an inner need, in turns a drive and a desire.

Although it is possible to imagine that this change from childhood to maturity might have come about easily and smoothly, in my case difficulties had to be faced, problems had to be solved and hardships had to be overcome. Adults in my vicinity were mostly immature and largely ignorant, hence their parental effect was minimal. Artworks were available but the use to be made of them had more to do with sensual pleasure than with enlightenment. As for that inner need, I can only say that in spite of it being misunderstood, falsified and rejected, it remained faithful and never left me in the lurch. My earliest work of maturation could be described as a justification of it.

I state without hesitation that meagre as was the parental and enlightenment influence due to artworks and mature adults, without it this need, this desire, would still be operative in me but mis-experienced by me as the cause of pain, of illness and mental turmoil; in short not as creative but destructive. In other words, the son of man must be raised. Children need to be brought up because they do not automatically grow up, to maturity, though they do become adults.

I would like it to be noticed that when I refer to this need, I do not mention a need for this or that. When, as a teenager, I expressed myself in terms of it, some help came my way but never the same way twice. 'You need to learn how to survive.' 'You need to be happy.' 'You need to fit in with society.' Once even: 'You need to join the army, that will straighten you out.'

Distraught as I was and in dire need of an explanation for this experienced need, I decided to pay the closest possible attention to how I perceived it. Where, exactly, were the nerve-endings, so to speak, that registered the malaise, the discomfort, the depression, not to mention the frequent switches from a pitiful lack of self-worth to a sense of absurd superiority and back again. I enclosed myself in a circle of solitude and set to work.

The outcome, or result of my efforts, was what I called 'the new body' and when I understood, really knew and understood, such a new body as mine, I realized that for once I was getting somewhere. I had redefined knowledge, in the sense that a body of knowledge, as made up of all I really and truly knew at a given time, was my own body.

This struck me as a revolutionary development, especially because it differed so radically from the one I had been led to expect by adults who had informed me that a body of knowledge was intellectually produced and stored in books. However I stuck to my guns, because for once I experienced that sense of constancy and establishment I had secretly craved. It was part of the central need alright. My newly discovered body of knowledge allowed me to be patient with others. You might say that I came out of my shell – not from one day to the next of course but perceptibly all the same. I had been totally mistaken about this sense apparatus of mine. Vision – sight, hearing, touch etc. had not until now connected to that complex realm whence all my needy dissatisfactions and insecurities seemed to originate. Now that they did, I gained courage for a great variety of undertakings. I was no longer – or let me say : I was less and less – in a quandary as to how best to secure an outward relation of consequence to my thoughts and this turned out to be very important. I was happy to let external relations and affinities, however disparate or causal, take care of themselves. Secretly I had suspected right from the start, that what really mattered was how, and whether or not, I personally perceived the world and not how various supposed and alleged parts of it fitted together. I suppose I felt that in spite of its chaotic or contradictory appearance at times, the world as such did not need me, nor anyone else for that mater, to correct it. I was confirmed in this opinion by my steadily growing body of knowledge and by the way that, in tandem with this growth, a world increasingly revealed itself to me as true and beautiful. And that was the one that interested me, not the disproportionate and disorienting world, which little by little receded into the background, evidently insubstantial.

It wasn't long before it occurred to me that this world newly known by me and thereby contributing to my body of knowledge was none other than the world of my childhood but now perceived awarely. My response to this insight was both sorrow and joy. I had regained my paradise but what a pity that first I had lost it!

Piece by piece the early faculties were renewed and installed. Dream, wonder, reverence all reintroduced themselves

– or rather properly introduced themselves, in the sense that they revealed to me their names and qualities.

Before long I thought of this as religion. I had never embraced or rejected religion as a concept. My small familiarity with denominations and churches had never been fortunate or comfortable. I had always decided that substance was lacking. The root and heart of my human being were never addressed, remained untouched. At the same time the degree of popularity of various orthodox or sectarian movements puzzled me. In various guises and disguises I had asked, both myself and others: What exactly is religion? What does it mean, what is it like, to be religious? Are some religions more useful than others?

I imagined then that I had a fair indication of the answer when, thanks to my new body, my body of knowledge, I was permitted to recapture the values and qualities of my childhood – perhaps of childhood as such.

*

My curiosity about 'religion', especially while I imagined that the concept might suitably be made to refer to what I was experiencing as this return to child-reality, led me to the Christian Gospels. I thought of them as Christian because the Christian Religion, an organized body of dogma, in a sense does lay some sort of claim to them. What I discovered, to my surprise, as I read these four documents, was that in them, especially in the three 'synoptic Gospels', breathes a spirit I could not identify in Christianity except as a mere shadow. The spirit I refer to emanated not from the words themselves, which seemed more or less to be bland reportage, but from the central figure that had given rise to them.

I sought the help of someone who had carefully looked into the history of this Jesus and of his time and who, especially in the light of eschatological expectation, made good

77

sense, for me, of much that had seemed puzzling, mysterious and even contradictory in those documents.

I came to the conclusion, that what really interested me was not the Christian Religion but the personality and teachings of this central figure of the Gospels.

It appeared that much of what he was reported to have said would apply, according to him, not so much to his present time but to the time after his death, when something like a new reality, not hitherto fully apprehended, would commence. At first this struck me as mysterious. I could not imagine how reality could alter, from one age to the next.

By this time I had experienced various upheavals in my own life. Their effect on me was sometimes disorienting but always to an extent comprehensible. It seemed that, along with new physical and mental experience, also arrived new perception and understanding. The way I had been instructed by society in general and school in the particular was no use to me whatsoever and in the end more of a hindrance that I had to unlearn. I had to educate myself, to withdraw from those extinct teachings, and I was able to do it in terms of what was given to me to perceive and understand, directly or indirectly, in response to that central, elemental, inborn need in me.

Under all those circumstances it seemed wise to refer to what I had lost and was gradually regaining as my human nature. That was live. In comparison, what I had to come out of and rid myself of was extinct. It 'stuck out', remained merely external, with no conceivable connection to my physical health and wholeness, which after all originated inwardly.

I came round very gradually to the realization that the existence of a new reality here and now made sense to me because otherwise my most formative experience should have been rejected.

Now it's one thing being grateful for having learned something new but its quite another coming to the conclusion that literally everything worth knowing and experiencing has to be new. It gives a new flavour to what 'new' means.

The fact (what I believed to be a fact) that this new reality I was learning had been available for a couple of millennia did not imply that it had always and everywhere since then been known and accepted. If it was really of an elemental nature, as I assumed it must be, to account for its various effects on me, then surely, while knowledge of it would be a blessing, ignorance of it was bound to be something like a curse. I could not help wondering if perhaps the increasingly global upheavals of the past two thousand years might be explained in terms of this curse. At the same time, one knew of isolated cases where the blessing seemed to have been quite dramatically exemplified. There was no reason to suppose that either the curse or the blessing was necessarily tied to traditional Christianity, which lent itself as readily to mayhem as to merit.

It was not without an appreciable degree of trepidation that I realized I had my work cut out for me. It seemed up to me to define even my own ethic of work. That same need that had in turns plagued and fired me turned, in terms of what I was willing to work out and personally exemplify, into a masterful source of truthful information. The prophetic aspect of it I was willing to play down. What I came to mean by creativity, this became my mainstay.

*

Now the illusion of the mythic had always fascinated me. Why, in some areas of knowledge, was it so important that we rely solely on inspiration? Or put it this way: Why, at times, was there no way forward except on the wings of pure inspiration? The creative impulse no longer originated in flesh and blood but straight from 'the brain'. I do mean 'the' brain, not my brain. 'The brain', I found out, is a wonderful conception. It wasn't all that long ago when I wrote an essay on 'the' human brain and during the course of it I learned this and that.

But I am getting ahead of myself. What I do want to draw attention to here is precisely this 'what we can learn' when we access 'the human brain' – by means of our own brain, of course. Pure inspiration – or mythic content, as we might also call it – embedded in flesh and blood, now that is the secret of masterful creation.

By that I don't mean to suggest that masterful creation is nothing but this. No, I say it's the secret. It's important to know how to get on with secrets. They secrete themselves, if you get what I mean. In other words there is that about reality that is secret and the creative process reveals it, in masterful fashion.

Masterful creation now and again needs to rely directly on the 'deus abscondicus'. The Jesus of the Gospels seems to refer to this when he says that no one can see god except that the son of man has revealed him to him. But let's not get into theology. At present I only want to mention how this difference between direct or pure inspiration and the more deliberate and reflective sort impressed itself on me. At first I was so swamped by pure inspiration that I could manage nothing else. The works that stem from that time are quite 'incomprehensible'. I am tempted to say that reason played no role, but then role-playing reason is not the only sort. You can think the works of pure inspiration but you cannot think about them. They make no sense except to the inner eye, and where the inner eye is missing, consternation is the result. They can be 'hard sayings' that arrive via 'the' spirit. Or – 'the' human brain speaks wisdom not accessible to your or my brain but – only to ours, in communion, in communality.

That was the break-through we just made there, did you notice? The spirit as such speaks directly to the community and not to the individual mind. I am not quite sure yet but I believe that's a crucial insight. You might put it this way: For pure inspiration, individuality is not enough; personality is required. We know by now that when we speak of a person we mean a human being not by him- or herself, as when we mean an individual, but in relation to one or more other human beings.

We don't go far wrong if, when we think of human beings and more precisely of personal human being, we have something like an achievement in mind. If we are not careful – by which I mean full of care rather than just cautious – we turn into mere individuals. We slide into that. If we don't catch ourselves on, we become individualists, in which case our personality – or personality itself – is not just dormant in us but extinct. Hopefully this extinction is temporary, however one can become attached to it, like to a morbid pleasure.

As a creative human being – which is to say as a human being – I know that I need to be challenged now and again, or more precisely that my individuality needs to be challenged, so that I do not decline into mere individualism, into egotism. And by the way, I am not altogether certain that the true nature of personality, which requires maturity, is all that widely known. Most of us are far too much persuaded by a need for a lively individualism, while personality and communality, the reality of those who truly live and have life, is at best neglected, at worst feared. There is a kind of psyched up individuality to which we admiringly refer as charisma – which proves that we need our heads examined. Some popular preachers mistakenly rely on such charisma in their efforts to 'raise the dead' as it were, but the dead in reaction to it only become charismatic, or intensely individualistic.

Enough of that. What I would like to stress is the need now and again, or rather the requirement, for pure spirit and for the effects of pure inspiration. Perhaps what I mean by pure here should be explained a little more. Certainly pure does not mean clean as compared to dirty, but something like 'not yet embedded in ethical living' – with the emphasis most decidedly on the 'not yet'.[1]

At the same time, by spirit I do not mean any old spirit but the merciful spirit of love. This spirit may be perceived or 'heard', by him who has ears to hear it.

The perceiving or 'hearing' of this spirit however right away implies a recording of what is perceived, in a language of one sort or another, such as human speech.

Thereafter commences the embedding, or incorporation, in ethical living. The desire for ethical living in the one who is to perceive this spirit is essential, otherwise the result is falsified and is called raving. Where this desire for ethical living exists, however, this spirit may be truly perceived or 'heard'.

I have mentioned above that the definitive effect or purpose of this spirit is communal, so in order to be able to perceive it, I must be willing to share what I hear. Not only is this spirit communal, in form, but also ethical, in content. Not only do we want to share what we hear but we also know that what we want to share is useful and good.

Initially he who perceives is not aware of this difference between form and content, for he perceives like a child, in simplicity and trust. Just as we, as human beings, begin as implicitly trusting children and as we grow up and are brought up

---

[1] We have to be careful of those who popularize pure spirit as some prestigious angelic or ideal quantity, in other words as 'pure spirit in itself' or 'as such' to which bereft individuals may dedicate their fragile egos and devote their timid selves; a kind of Naziism of the spirit.

we become aware, so does a mature adult, if he is able to 'hear' this merciful spirit of love, first accept it in perfect simplicity and trust and as time passes he is able to ponder and articulate it in more and more awareness.

There is no need to be 'born again' if we grew up and were brought up 'properly'. If a child is brought up to awareness in the light of merciful spirit, then what else can that mean except that he has life and that he has it in abundance? As mature human beings however, we measure ourselves constantly against that infusion of merciful spirit that always keeps us to the mark. We learn continually to be the truth, to adjust, by our works, to the demands that are made on us by that spirit and to adapt to the reality that is constantly changing.

Gone are the days when part of us was dead and the other part stressed. Especially our appetites have changed. That original need, which was masked by so much happiness and sadness, is now being satisfied. We imbibe and ingest the beauty and truth of the world.

*

Alas, how much does that last statement not need to be qualified! The beauty and truth of the world indeed? Who would have thought it, when depravity, degeneracy and perversion fill our newspapers!

However since when are newspapers a reflection of the real world? Are they not themselves part and parcel of it? Then what exactly do we mean by the real and the unreal world? By real and unreal society, community, personality and so on?

How suddenly our visual apparatus closes down, as if we were no longer conscious of our surroundings! We become inwardly aware and our being is refreshed. Is it not as if from one moment to the next we had left the outside world behind, while coming into contact with our own inspirited flesh and blood? World still exists and now we no longer speak of 'the' world. It makes no sense to speak of 'the world', as of self-contained, finite being. What we mean now, by world, well, there is no end to it. Is it not as if suddenly we had come home? Gone is the exposure of our flesh and blood to evil influences. An existential comfort and convenience is ours.

Is it not as if we had participated at a meal? One moment the world is attractive. The next moment we are satisfied and fulfilled in 'world'.

We do well to familiarize ourselves with this matter and manner of means. Are we then never to be hungry and thirsty again?

One moment world attraction; the next moment world fulfilment. What could be more desirable, more satisfactory, for that essential, human natural need of ours!

I know it sounds as if we were eating and drinking beautiful and true world. Well, what if it were so? For most of the time we are active and passive wherever we are. We pay no particular attention to our environment as such, nor to our inward being. We live and we have life. Nothing can surpass that. We do our work, we play with our children. We socialize and communicate.

Suddenly our surroundings open out. No need for excitement, nonetheless we notice something like an appetite, like a willingness to achieve or an openness to occasion and event. There may also be some reluctance to overcome, like a surly mood, an onset of weakness. Never mind. Let us rise – to this occasion. Is there ever really a shortage of occasions for us to rise to? Even the most indifferent moment carries a message. Whenever we envision life, do we really feel we are up to it?

If we refer to the most ordinary experience, it is still experience and therefore it may be ingested.

An ingestion of experience! Now there we have a notion that obviates the sensational and the extraordinary.

I mean something very specific here. How ever we experience our inward or outward being, be it ever so trivial and boring, ever so puzzling or wondrous, chaotic or static, it may be ingested by us.

Mind you, we may have to incorporate a new organ first, but then what, if not that, are we about here!

So locate yourself first, know where and how you are, then understand (stand under) your state, your situation, your condition – your environment. If you are able to know and understand, do it now.

Or let's put it this way: World, inasmuch as you are able to perceive it right now, is substantial and you may take in that substance. As I said, the organ for this has to be developed. Thought is the prime developmental factor.

I am speaking entirely from practical experience right now. Also, you are not to suppose that some esoteric insight is required before, previous to, your acquisition of this organ. Esoteric insight, yes, if you like, but then right away as you ready yourself, with the result of a merciful consequence.

What you are asking for here is a taste and a stomach for reality. Actually at the moment I am asking for you, in the hope that you attend me.

So your attitude, as the attitude of the one who asks, is of course courteous. In other words you do not try to make anything happen, by force or some instrumentality. Ask with all the willpower at your disposal but keep in mind that the response has to come in its own good time.

85

We probably underestimate the power of thought. Once we have decided on the spirit with authority, our thought is organic and we no longer need to spend time with experimentation. It is now a case of willing, thinking and perceiving all in one. You might say that we will to think, we think to perceive and we perceive world.

Our individual personality is now finally intact. We are no longer merely a conduit for spirit and we assert ourselves in the true sense of the word. We do not assert our opinions or our rights but ourselves. This takes a while to confirm. If anyone were to ask us now why we behave as we do, we would be able to say that our behaviour is sanctioned and that we have no particular reasons for our behaviour except those we invent for expediency's sake.

*

With this new attitude that we have to experience, and to the experience of world-environment in the particular, also comes our fullest possible sense of responsibility for truly ethical behaviour. Our living becomes consequential. The notion of experience as digestible food is no longer so strange for us. Knowledge is not only head and heart knowledge but also stomach knowledge. We are learning how to ingest and how to imbibe the spirit that has 'poured itself out over all flesh'. We are developing a proper organ for that. The exercise of that organ, or rather the activity of it, becomes a most satisfactory sideline of our work-orientation. Needless to say we will wish to make this possible for others, however all too often we come up against the most adamant unwillingness, so that eventually we decide to make do, by demonstrating and exemplifying. We show who we are and we leave it at that. If it happens that someone shows an interest, then we can always test the ground to decide what might be able to stand on it and not sink down or fall over.

If I look back now to how I was as a child, before my head was filled with materialistic notions and my heart was stultified by those around me who had traded in their human-natural affection for popularity and prestige, I can well remember how immediately and how innately I experienced my surroundings; how it utterly satisfied me to make the acquaintance of a blue gentian flower, for example, so that even at the age of five I wanted to draw it and paint it so that others might know it too – if I recall this to mind I have no difficulty in understanding why, during the intervening years, I have been able to remain true to that knowledge and that all efforts to mislead me, by those who had no such knowledge, merely served to solidify my certainty and to justify my faith.

* * * * *

The Family of Man

We say of someone: He is a family man. At other times we speak of the family of man. The generous interpretation of 'family' would have us content ourselves with the father – mother – child constellation. When we optimistically say that all men are brothers we may not have any intention of deluding ourselves over our actual, everyday experience of the one next to us. Meanwhile a search in ourselves may very well produce some human natural affinity for all human beings, whether we know them, know of them or do not yet know them.

A priceless advantage is to be gained, once we have decided we prefer existence over non-existence, by contemplating the depth, breadth and extension of human relation independent of sex, skin colour, creed, etc. Down that road, if we care to take it, we come across such hindrances as would convict us of a variety of shortcomings, largely in terms of our personality but also with respect to our diverse habits of thought and feeling, either inherited or acquired. As a consequence we like to leave that concept 'family of man' fairly empty. Our own family, if we have been lucky enough to experience what might cheerfully pass for one, has hopefully given us, or is presently giving us, some useful insight into what is to be gained by a very particular kind of affection, that does not so much depend on liking but rather on voluntary and intentional love.

*

We are caught up in an agony of worldliness, if our search in ourselves produces nothing but reasons for surviving. These are all honed to perfection if we live in an environment that is devoid of true art and culturally dedicated to the amassing of property and safeguarding of liberty. The individual's desire for independence from others drowns out in him any vestige of emotion, while the lasting effect of comparative status and prestige hobbles even the young as they strive to make sense of the shocking disregard for eternal values by their parental elders.

While society is seen, is experienced and studied, as a thing in itself, it impresses as nothing more than a safeguard of the continuity of popular interests. These, such as for example the everlasting preoccupation with property both carnal and intellectual or with the pictorial landscape of things, will continue to titillate the modern mind until kingdom come, there is no way of getting around that. However our direst expectations cannot come near to what would ensue if this were all to life. Happily there is more that is of value, even in the most primitive tribal organization, than such a view of an inverted society can bring to our attention. At the same time we know of certain influences that civilization brings to bear, which would eventually undermine even the most rudimentary relations between individuals, if countervailing forces from within those individuals, in terms of instinctive passions and emotions, did not repeatedly draw attention to the need for checks and balances in the name of orderly thought as presented by a few more enlightened members of the population. I count, among those influences, the notion of superficial manners, customs and rules for the sake of the sort of ideological straightjacket that every now and again is fashioned due to the fear that this inturned society may not be permanent. Of course it cannot be permanent, but that is not because not enough effort is being made in that direction by the powers that be, but rather because there is more to human being than such a flawed perception of human relationship can supply for us.

Perhaps due to a mishap or after a series of false starts, the accumulated dissatisfaction with the status quo backfires. To some it seems like a short-circuit in the thought processes that have for so long been taken for granted, when suddenly the world stands on its head and a most peculiarly fatalistic mood causes some poor individual to break out in a sweat and shout:

"Enough!" He might not even know who it was that shouted. Besides, enough of what? Perhaps he had not been thoroughly enough inoculated against original thought and feeling. Who can say. It's a comparataive thing. In any case, it seems he harbours a lifetime's resentment against those who should have informed him of the fact that not everything that makes you cross is worth rejecting; that rehabilitation after rejection by Society (sic) is well worth it; that the supernatural explanations of a nature that excludes human nature are not worth a tinker's. He withdraws for forty days into the desert – or into a cave – to digest the manna from heaven that has finally managed to break through that shell called 'social responsibility', 'duty to Society', 'modern taste', in short, the status quo. I mean the status quo in terms of every conceivable faculty and function of 'the human being'.

When he eventually surfaces, everything around him looks different. All the details are finely honed and ultimately significant. Father and mother, sister and brother, although they stand right next to him, appear to be miles away. What seems close to him is something about himself, something like a protective covering or a selective sensitivity. The language that comes to mind when he decides to interact with someone next to him shimmers like a two-edged sword. When he speaks, some fly into a fury, others walk away, supremely puzzled. There's not much he can do about that. If he clams up for too long, his general wellbeing suffers, to say the least.

We call this the birth of true personality. Out of it is born true community.

*

If the family we were brought up in was social in the sense that our personal liberty was thwarted due to an insistence on the profligacy of the human heart, where whatever we do or

90

contemplate doing has to fit into some reasonable category or there's hell to pay, then our capacity for coping within an open or liberal social setting is almost nil. You might say that we have to learn to trust our heart impulses. The so-called profligate heart is no longer to frighten us. We are no longer to reject the uncomfortable thoughts that inform us of the fact that our resources are perhaps very limited when it comes to true human relationship.

Not that the concept 'true human relationship' has any meaning for us yet. Truth, until now, has been much more of an appetite than a satisfaction. At any rate, we long for that satisfaction now and sense within ourselves the presence of one or two faculties for the appropriation of new intelligence, that promises to stay with us once we have it. Until now we have not been able, really, to make any knowledge our own, because it was always eminently forgettable, being either of the head or of the heart, either emotional or intellectual.

The fact that we now can make physical sense is bound to alter our approach, intentional or otherwise, to our fellow man.

At first we have something to give but no one to give it to. Also, the language we customarily made use of will no longer let us make use of it but it seems to have an agenda of its own.

We bear with this and learn how to be creative. At first, what a relief! We can say what we wish to say without concerning ourselves over a backlash. What we are really coming up with, is a social contact that lays no claims to the other person's agreement. Neither of course are we merely expressing ourselves, considering our steady co-operation with being beyond our control. If we speculate as to the nature of this being, we may be vouchsafed some answers but the important thing is to engage and impart, whatever our chosen medium.

*

The discovery that society is an option and not a burden can never come too early. After all it was only presented to us as a burden by the unimaginative guardians of the status quo. Now we begin to realize that even the status quo is nothing to be afraid of. The spirit of knowledge has entered our veins. We are well advised to make ready for surprises.

The thing is that once we are no longer afraid of society, we are leaving it behind.

This time the journey is open-eyed and not shocking. We experience an intimacy that makes us smile at the social constraints and the social advantages. Reason has begun to teach us how to be ourselves, without being timid or heavy-handed and we are willing, for once, to perform our tasks in the light of day, because here only 'the right sort' can appreciate our accomplishments. We experience the communal tact.

Community grows quietly and emotionally all around us. We refer to our communal environment. We can now step in and out of social arrangements and attachments with knowing ease. We begin to make sense of 'our' community and we realize, almost with a sense of foreboding, that we cannot step out of it and still call it – what? A community? The community? No such thing. Our community promises mysterious ties, mysterious bonds and contacts. It reaches into the past and into the distance. Members of my community are those I trust, here or gone. We communicate, in signs, words, gestures or spirit. I perform my tasks for the members of my community and not for anyone else.

Is this like saying if I am a painter I paint for those who like my paintings? Add to that the members of my family, my friends and acquaintances, and that is my community? What's mysterious about that? Those who know me and whom I know – would that do? Or what about the sum-total of all those whom I wish well?

But human beings don't wish anyone ill. We don't see eye to eye with everyone but that doesn't mean we don't wish them well.

A closer approximation to what I mean by community becomes possible when I apply to my specific personality. As a person, I bring my unique individuality to bear on 'those around me' and I can only do this creatively – in other words in line with what I perceive to be truthful, which necessarily involves a readiness and willingness to ignore what I like or dislike.

What I must watch now is that my community – those with whom I communicate – does not turn into 'a' community. That would betoken a slide into comparative ignorance. As soon as my community becomes identifiable from without, I am no longer communicating creatively and before long, unless I repair this situation, I will be a member of a society and very likely incur a variety or privileges for no other reason than that 'I belong', that 'I am a member.' At all costs, this is to be avoided.

So before we go any further, let's acknowledge that just as the progress from society to community, so also the extension of myself from community to something greater must be entertained by me at least as a possibility and probability. For the moment we will not ask what this 'something greater' is, so that we can pay still more attention to what is essential about social and communal being.

*

We need to be in agreement about the undesirability of that 'worldly agony', as we called it earlier, where our basic need for carnal survival is forever at odds with our truthful feeling that there must be something better on the cards, else why were we born. That is what I mean by the agony. It's no use drawing the alleged fate of 'ancient man' or the predicament of 'the modern individual' into any comparison with what has to make sense to us here as the unfortunate and pitiable duality of stomach and brain, or, as some would put it, as the contradiction between our upper and lower halves, between our left and our right. Ancient man had his cults and those who seek solace in that direction nowadays are not able to delude themselves for long. The ancient indulgence is no longer viable. The modern individual tries to solve his existential problem by dividing himself into private and public, which makes for only a tentative and ultimately elusive peace.

Contemporary men and women finally realize, that total wholeness and healing is possible and so they take steps to liberate themselves from that worldly agony by espousing the freedom of being, or free being, and taking full advantage of any historic benefits that have become available in the realm of merciful spirit.

*

Perhaps we need to remind ourselves, that the worldly agony we might find ourselves in, is something that has happened and something we have allowed to come about and perhaps we have even confirmed it, though surely out of ignorance, otherwise who would choose to be stiff-necked and flint-hearted if he were aware of the pleasures of a blissful soul and of tender human being. In other words we do not find ourselves in this agony from birth. On the other hand, if we have been left to our own devices and not brought up or raised, as we say, we find ourselves in a predicament, because our childhood will have been wasted and our adulthood will be immature. So the son of man must be raised. Our humanity has to be helped along through infancy, childhood and youth in such a way that we grow to maturity. In the absence of an upbringing we fall by the wayside and even society is something we vaguely sense but we cannot participate because we lack the ability to associate, which is to say: to bring personality to bear on others, even for no other reason than to persuade ourselves of any meaning for our loneliness.

The actual and hellish experience of worldly agony however is reserved for adults, because they, unlike infants, children and youths, are responsible for themselves and for the condition of their human nature. They can only be helped by mature adults and their example and works, however it is up to themselves to seek that help and make the best of it. If help is available but it is not sought out, nothing can be done. Laughable and sad at once are the efforts of those who not only drag the horse to the water but also want to force it to drink. A pang of conscience right away reminds me of my own early laughable and sad parental efforts in that direction. Happily, since parenting is an activity of the mature, we get to practice for the rest of our lives.

*

Once again, I distinguish between people and human beings, between popularity and humanity. The distinction applies only to adults, inasmuch as adults are responsible for themselves.

We are human while we seek to grow towards and in maturity. We are popular while we do not. The accent here is on the seeking. Children may be so neglected that their human nature has withdrawn. To all intents and purposes they are no longer human but with parenting from mature adults their human being may be brought into focus again. They can never be said to be popular however because the initiative for growth is not available to them but only to adults.

Language itself reveals some of the difference between human beings and people. I can call someone a human being but not a people. It is the growth-initiative that supplies the identity, which in turn can be supplanted by any interest in popularity.

As people, we continually try to produce for ourselves an Ersatz-identity by associating in terms of some myth, such as the country, the nation, the race or dogma myths such as anti-Semitism or philistinism, and this gives us some semblance of a fake hold on our existence for the time being. It is not surprising that the various types of genocide are perpetrated by people who dimly sense that there is such a thing as a difference between primary and secondary value, while their disappointment and resentment at not enjoying the real thing, i.e. humanity, human nature and human being, turns into vitriolic hatred and murderous intent against some group they define as an underclass or they vilify them and hold them responsible for any evil under the sun. Typically, it is those who themselves are not human who indulge in the perverse luxury of accusing others of this condition.

However we do not need to reach for extremes. Any human being who slides into popularity shows this by right away criticizing or prejudging someone. By pointing to the speck in someone else's eye, we conveniently blind ourselves to the beam in our own.

It stands to reason, therefore, that our first response to any popularity we detect in ourselves must be reflection and repentance, as we try to re-establish ourselves in our human being.

We do well to let rank be 'good-spiritual', not worldly or social. (I use the term 'good-spiritual' in the awareness that not all spirit is good.)

*

When all is said and done, it should not be hard to imagine the birth of society and association out of fear in the face of an eternal recurrence of that worldly agony we have discussed. Flights of terror, onsets of horror, proverbially drive us into the arms of anyone else who knows that fear. We associate, we choose to associate, in the hope of some relief from the lively insecurity that besets us at unpredictable times. The unpredict-ability turns out to be especially nerve-racking. More and more, as we begin to seek the society of others like ourselves, that all too familiar world agony becomes more bearable and less of a threat. If we should ever personally find ourselves at this low level of existence where even the merest sociability becomes appreciable in the event of an agonizing world ex-perience, we will never again be over-critical of those who cling to every shred of available society, even at the expense of any progress to a familiarity with a communal existence. Equally it becomes understandable, that before they relinquish their hold on that safety net, they will need to be shown that a. something better is possible and b. that an artificially pro-longed social relationship cannot last.

Knowledge of each most commonly plays into the decision to try something a little less fear-based and a little more re-warding.

When society 'sickens', as it is sometimes called, we tend to bolster our relationships, by inventing new regulations and tightening the rules. We do this 'for everyone' then, because we cannot imagine that anyone would be so silly as to veto any further degree of social security. Custom, duty, tradition and law are all drawn increasingly into the equation, even as we begin to sense here, especially in the presence of some who reject or shrug off the time-honoured social values, that this restlessness to move on, however we experience it, in our-selves or from others, is really something quite different from the horror and terror in the face of world agony.

This restlessness to move on is not at all based on fear. It stems rather from a frequently quite emotional recognition that 'the old values will not hold'. The accompanying emotion might be anything from loathing and disgust to a feeling of being supremely dissatisfied with what we now are liable to call 'the status quo'.

Happily our father's dispensation accounts for many mansions. There are always at least a few who set us an example of communality and quite possibly they have never had to come face to face with the world as agonistic experience. How delighted they are, when their communal being is enriched by an introduction once again to someone who has been there and has come away, albeit restlessly, with a fresh take on the value of community and a refreshing contribution to make to a community that has perhaps grown somewhat self-satisfied and stale.

Most of the social rules and regulations, not to mention the so-called social values, are extemporized. They are invented for the occasion. As social beings, we try to cope as best we can, in the knowledge of that terrifying, horrifying alternative that 'does not bear thinking about'.

This extemporized nature of all that is socially, and only socially, binding is also what causes the loathing and the rage in the one who has what it takes to step into communal relationships.

One can never repeat often enough, however, that this so-called step can only be taken by one person at a time. While a society is properly made up of individuals, who are willing to think alike to the extent of some corporate social gains, progress into community implies a developing personality. No political movement, no ideology, can confer personality for the one who experiences, often painfully, the comparative limitations and constraints of society where it is presented as the final form of human growth. Where a social individual is enraged by his world and overcome by the desire to change it – and when has there ever been such a widespread wish to 'change the world' as nowadays! – let him be informed that what is at stake is his or her own growth into a communal realm of existence and all that that entails. To the extent that he undertakes to affect and perhaps even infect others with his dissatisfaction he will only raise havoc in the end.

*

It does make sense to speak of American society or English society, because there we refer to particular styles of behaviour as accepted by a major portion of a population as geographically defined. More specifically, we may arrive at some notion of the social relations of some Plains Apache tribes during the eighteenth century in what is now Oklahoma. Culture and society reflect one upon the other. Whether society is tribal, civic, politically conscious to some degree, all this, if we wish to study societies, will play into our estimation and interpretation of how a group of people, large or small, dealt or deal with their fears, their horrors and terrors, in the face of agonistic world experience. While we ourselves are still primarily social beings, we cannot really speak intelligently about societies. However we can try to come to grips with our own in some hopefully charitable effort to move on to an understanding of ourselves as communal beings. Again, this would be one individual's struggle to be no longer influenced by the fear of lapses in his social order or of break-downs in his social security. It can never be a concerted effort by some or several individuals. The true, communal personality of each, by definition, has to be formed by each in his or her own way.

People will also form societies, such as a society for the prevention of cruelty to children or animals, and their reason for this will be a more specific, more aimed effort to ameliorate fearful actions in others. So one could imagine a society for the prevention of cannibalism or for the encouragement of greater sociability. Always there would be this consciousness of risk and danger in the absence of society.

If we were to learn about society and social behaviour in that light, we would be in a much better position, when our time comes, to step into that inner and more noble order of being, based not on fear but on faith.

*

We are born with faith and there is no reason why we should ever be without it. However we lose it and then we are afraid.

If we do not lose faith, we do not have a notion as to the social behaviour of those who do. Social behaviour and faithful behaviour are worlds apart. Those whose faith is intact can, however, understand the behaviour of members of society, in terms of 'there but for the grace of god go I'. They have learned, hopefully even in their youth, that faith is a gift with which we are born and which remains with us through use and application, so on one hand they have reason to be proud for having nourished their faith through action and sanctified their action through faith. On the other hand, when they see how those who lack faith or who have a pretend faith get on, they cannot help but be angry and disappointed, for a potential life in community is lost to them.

When a faithful person comes across a social individual who demonstrates by his behaviour his motivation by fear for his carnal security, by terror for his lawful behaviour and by horror for his gregarious conduct, his personal example in all those walks of life is what counts. What rises to the surface in spectacular fashion, when faith rubs shoulders with fear, is a supreme confidence in the light of day. This confidence is what touches both parties. By the faithful one, it is celebrated and praised, while by the social one it is admired and desired. Everything else we can think of that might speak for good influence by the faithful one on the social one is subsumed by this supreme confidence. Nothing needs to be said, nothing needs to be done. Which is not to ignore that some are born to teach and some to preach. All the same, unless they do so in this supreme confidence – which does not arise unless they 'rub shoulders' with the faithless ones – their teaching and preaching is for nothing.

*

If we have faith, that is our strong suit. It means we believe that our human nature will always see us through. We can even leave god as a distinct entity out of it because we believe that all that is is good. However god is the guarantor of our personhood, so that by having faith in god we advance beyond having faith and stopping there.

It is impossible to have faith and not in god. Compare this to swimming and swimming in water. He who has faith has the lot. He who has faith in god has more. It depends on where and how we just find ourselves.

Personality implies that we take our individuality on faith. While we still need to keep the least hold on our individuality, always cruising close to shore, needing to let others know somehow that we exist, we have not yet risen into our person-hood.

A person in his own right knows and believes that his individuality is intact and consequently he can assume the responsibility for the one next to him without losing faith or face. In the absence of faith he would fear for himself, he would be afraid of losing track of his self, his sensation of his thing-being, in which case he would also no longer be a complete person.

The incomplete person periodically hankers for sensation of his self, of his importance in the eyes of others, of his self-control, of his material independence and of his confidence based on his ability to shape his future. Nonetheless, better be an incomplete person than an individual.

The faith that allows us to deploy our personality to the full is ours from birth but lost due to improper, or lack of, upbringing. (Education during childhood and youth repairs that shortfall or it is not education.)

While faith is necessarily seen as doctrinal or denominational, being tied by definition to a religion, none of these arguments hold. Faith is either human natural or else to some extent encumbered. So it is not until we understand what is meant by human natural faith that we can begin to educate, either the young or ourselves.

A part of that understanding reveals to us how faith and community depend on each other and feed off each other. My desire to communicate will not be satisfied except I have sufficient faith and by the same token I can increase my faith by practicing to communicate.

Faith extends from our being, while communication is a species of doing. In community both are involved.

It is easy to see now how the social habits, the social rules and regulations, need no longer concern the man of faith. They concern the man of fear. Nonetheless the man of faith will 'rub shoulders' with the man of fear. He will not seek him out, neither will he avoid or reject him. He does not choose his company but neither will he shun him. The man of faith is either strengthened due to this accidental intercourse or he is no longer a man for faith. The man of faith is either encouraged or annihilated. This is what happens. It is not done, the way men of a false or artificial faith have in the past set out to annihilate those of a differently false faith, in the hope of strengthening their case. Indeed theirs was and always is a society, and their social aim is to deal with the fear at the core of

102

their being by agitating for increased numbers. Do we see any of this nowadays?

*

As faith increases due to use and application during the communal interplay of persons among individuals in society, we can begin to speak of the power of faith. This is available to mature adults, who have shown and proven by their behaviour, that they are incapable of unethical behaviour. In other words, unless they can do good, they do nothing, in the knowledge that even by non-action or simple being they make a useful contribution to their community.

Once our faith is powerful, we are always responsible for it. What opens out in front of us now is a realm of activity in which all of creation is significantly related to us. Powerful faith brings that significance to our attention and allows us to operate in terms of it. For the first time now we become seriously aware of our creative faculty as a personal skill in the light of day. Creative spirit no longer just steps into situations where it is needed and where we have engaged on the basis of it in the certain hope of its leadership and co-operation. Now we have it so to speak in our power and it has us in its power; there is really no difference.

This power of belief allows us to change our environment in order to make it more suitable for our purpose and at the same time, in the name of it, we may change ourselves, in order to adapt more successfully to our eternal environment.

It occurs to us now that creative spirit is personal. It has its own agenda and we are more than willing to fit in with it. We learn how to apply ourselves, to whatever, in its name, so when we look around, we can find no better name for it than Jesus the Christ. Some slight history of this person may be known to us but what really counts is that we are aware of this resurrection spirit within us, where it has been since we were born but now for the first time we understand how it works.

Let us first look at what the purpose is of that spirit within us which has been guiding our actions and stimulating our behaviour since our mature adulthood.

We have known for some time that humanity is the essence of being. We are now able to describe humanity as merciful spirit. Merciful spirit informs all that is.

At the same time, we know that not all that is does. Unless it does, it cannot exist in the light of day. It is the universal law that all that is shall exist in the light of day. Only by means of a powerful faith can we grasp that.

Now that not only merciful spirit is within us but also resurrection spirit named Jesus the Christ, we may initiate such creative acts as bringing merciful spirit, or god, into the light of day.

Every human beings' great joy is to be able to initiate such acts and to bring them to fruition. We do so by laying down our life and afterwards picking it up again.

God is nameless but the resurrection spirit, the one we were wont to call the creative spirit, goes by the name of Jesus the Christ.

*

How annoying, how embarrassing for our ego, that we need someone else to assist us in putting these finishing touches on our world system! On the other hand, how fortunate for us, that someone exists and lives who makes it possible for us to appreciate unsystematic world order on the whole!

The discovery that Jesus the Christ lives and that the historical Jesus lives again, as the Christ, solves for the thinking and caring man a crucial problem. He says: Thank God that this has been done, otherwise I would have to try to do it myself and I know I would fail miserably.

The progress from ourselves in the possession of our human natural faith to the discovery of the Jesus who lived and now lives again is smooth and even. Alas, for how long, for how many years, is anyone in the possession of his human natural faith! Or perhaps we should point to this small matter of possession and acknowledge in the peace and quiet of our little chamber that the faith with which we were born and which we may well have taken for granted for a while was not on that account in our possession. Were we perhaps all too soon eager to possess *things* instead?

So there you have it. How soon did we not become possessive of things and gradually our faith slipped out of our hands; if it was ever in our hands. We have to be careful how we think about this, because the Christian Jesus is preached as having to come again and meanwhile those who believe in him lead at best moral lives, as did those who lived prior to the day of his transubstantiation.

Happily there are always a few to whom it is given to experience the entire dissatisfaction due to a modern life, halfway between faith as a gift and faith as a possession, so that they may search for the son of man.

*

The concept 'the family of man' is itself unfamiliar to us in its sense as a collective noun. Very likely we do not refer to 'the family of man' except in metaphoric fashion, and that is where we show our ignorance of what it is that causes all human beings to congregate, for no other reason than to be in contact for the sake of loving one another.

Why do we love one another? Since our humanity is merciful spirit and since human being is our main interest, is it any wonder that what worries us most is the lack of other human beings to love?

We might search for days without finding another and yet we know we must love nevertheless. Why must? Because we do not readily choose to do so. While we choose to do so there is neither compulsion nor constraint.

Now there is good reason for using the word 'family' in this context. We know that all human beings have within them merciful good spirit as their essential humanity. This spirit allows itself to be called father or mother.

What we are looking at now, however, are heaven-on-earth relationships. There is no reason why we should not be able to come up with the courage to think and speak in terms of heavenly earth and earthly heaven.

Consequently when we mean our earthly father or our earthly mother we right away also mean merciful good spirit. Not to do so would diminish our humanity and darken our life. Certainly no one wants that.

Heaven and earth, you see, are no longer separable, neither in thought nor in deed. Those who act and behave as if earth separately were a viable version of reality are as wide of the mark as those who try to imagine heaven separately.

When we mean our earthly son and daughter we right away also mean creative spirit, which allows itself to be called, named and imagined as the resurrected Jesus. Not to mean creative spirit diminishes our relationship to children.

We know that as mature adults we have a parental duty towards small children. Part of that duty would be every effort we make, by word of mouth or behaviour, to help raise those children to a realization that their earthily mothers and fathers bear within them merciful good spirit. Similarly our own parental duty is informed by that spirit.

Marriage in the old sense is no longer a viable proposition. It is unthinkable that when a mature man and woman get together to have a child they should not make the raising or upbringing of that child a priority for themselves.

Keep in mind that by the family of man we mean something very specific. Those who aim for it and realize it are not those who see social relationships as their be all and end all. At the same time those who have once had a taste of the communal relation will cheerfully go on to seek membership in the family of man.

In that same family, brotherhood, sisterhood and friendship are all open to those in whom the resurrection spirit is active, which is all human beings.

*

It is precisely due to this resurrection spirit, which is so openly active in the family of man, that at times we feel inclined to say: Nothing can harm us, for our wellbeing is secure. It is on account of our veritable experience of this spirit that we find ourselves positioned heart, mind and soul at the active and passionate centre of creation.

Well might one ask, why this should in any way be desirable. Surely it must be the results of creation that move us to expressions of approbation, of joy and delight. Also, if we ourselves should wish to be creative, how far can we afford to remove ourselves from the applause of an insightful audience?

In the family of man, the very air we breathe is creative. Nothing could be further from our apprehension than the existence of any dead matter. Conversation itself at once stimulates our appetite for more life and nourishes it with live substance.

Our appreciation of pain is such, that we never fall away from recognizing the element of renewal in it.

*

What interests us most in the family of man, is the human spirit, both creative and capable of resurrection. Each one of us may ask, and is wise to ask, sooner or later: What role does the human spirit play in my life? Evidently this is not a spirit that comes to us from beyond somewhere and surprises us in the act of trying to carry on without it. Most of all we would like to know how we can be more powerful, more capable of ethical action. In the family of man, asking this question implies an immediate answer, here and now. It is particular insights we are after at given moments under certain circumstances, in order to respond to a perceived need or so that we may initiate creative intervention in situations of crisis, both on our own behalf and on behalf of anyone else.

The human spirit is always whole. We do not ask for human spirit but for the human spirit. A single inward request is all that is required. At our disposal will then be the power to create and the power to resurrect. However we will not have this power in our power, in the sense that the human spirit dissolves into us or some such thing. Neither is it a case of cooperation, where this spirit and we ourselves both have a role to play during creation and resurrection. No, whenever we see fit, we ask for the human spirit and then we, so to speak, allow ourselves to be surprised. We do not stand back with our hands behind our back, merely awaiting things to come but we keep alive our initial reason for asking for the human sprit. What happens then is not something we could have planned or foreseen. Even as I write these sentences, when I come to the end of my tether I ask for this spirit and then, very likely, the next sentence comes to me. Or perhaps I turn away from my work and go for a bite to eat. What I do next will always be my decision even though, or because, this spirit is at the root of it. I am after all a human being, so the human spirit cannot ever be alien to me, nor can I be at odds with it.

Neither of course is this human spirit not with me if I do not ask for it. We do well to keep our imagination in check here. The fact that at some given moment I ask for it does not imply that it had fled from me for a while.

*

Why is it important for us to ask for this spirit even though it never departs from us? Because by asking we demonstrate our readiness for its intervening action. How gloriously we become part of the creative process! How wonderfully the resurrection is active on our behalf!

We are members of this family for the sake of one another. This means that in terms of this human spirit, which we could also call the family spirit, we cannot go wrong. At times we are like sleep-walkers for a while, until we realize how orderly our conduct has been and how perfectly informed of the ethical right way.

Most grateful we are for the fact, that this spirit judges for us. No longer are we strung out between alternative possibilities, for as soon as we sense a predicament, we defer to this spirit and exercise our faculties afresh.

Of course there is a legitimate question as to the extent to which we may commit ourselves to anyone else's will. Love requires this frequently of us, that we delay our convictions and put off behaviour on the basis of them for the purpose of someone else's peace of mind. In the family of man, a brother or sister, a friend, a son or daughter, these all lay claim to our attention and demand that we willingly cooperate with their individual expression and personal presentation of themselves. In the absence of the human spirit we would soon be lost for words and deeds. In certain knowledge of the resurrection however we go out on limb after limb as if to provoke miracles.

In the beginning, when this spirit first reveals itself to us, we understandably proceed with caution. Always and again new habits need to be formed, we pass through experimental phases and learn how we can rely and how we must not impose ourselves, as if we lacked understanding.

Very gently then it takes us in hand and informs us of its blessings, which are truly a multitude.

The human or family spirit is ineffable. At first we are loath to admit as much but then we realize that we are to look not at it but for its results, its works and achievements. Indeed once we have called upon it we may observe the changes that take place.

* * * * *

The Power of Purpose

1

It's amazing, when we first realize how much we can accomplish – with pure intention. I don't mean mere intention but pure intention. Purpose and intention are not miles apart. The colloquial emphasis places purpose somewhat more outside ourselves, in the future and in front, whereas intention is generally seen as taking inward precedence. I intend to combine the two concepts and to use them interchangeably as I gradually narrow this inquiry down to an interest in the useful good we can do, powerfully, first of all without even stepping outside ourselves, empirically, for the purpose of impressing ourselves on the world or for changing the world according to our lights, and then also by influencing our environment, but more or less in exemplary fashion, coincidentally, rather than through forceful and direct interference. My emphasis will therefore be placed on the moral and ethical effectiveness of inward purposefulness and not initially on external choices, to which we are all too often driven in any case and then we come up with explanations and justifications afterwards – as if we had intended what should in all honesty be described as a happy accident. If things don't turn out right, we can always say: "That is not what I meant at all."

An understanding, at the outset, of the separateness of intention from execution, of purpose from result and reward, is crucial. A set purpose does not automatically imply, or guarantee, a practical performance. Neither does activity and business of every sort necessarily presuppose an intention or purpose. This separateness is a simple fact. Looking at the surface of it, we may well say: So what? However I intend to show – and to demonstrate – that a great deal hinges upon it. As with most simple facts, it matters what we make of them. A fact is like a piece of reality, a building block. It can be used or abused. It can also be completely ignored. The investment of a minimum of philosophic curiosity persuades me that much is to be gained, in this case, by not ignoring and then by using and not abusing.

A consciousness of history persuades me that, for the ancients, purpose and performance did not stand in the same relation. A close reading of documents, especially of a personal nature, seems to me to reveal an approach to the separability of the two, in the mind of course, and even a desire for success in that direction, but not until the Christian era is the actual separateness taken for granted, sometimes in the sense of something which cannot be mended but mostly as a development with potentially dangerous consequences. In theology, great emphasis is placed on the security of the realm of belief vis-à-vis the 'worldly' domain. It's as if the 'within' and the 'without' of the human being were both vying for independence and predominance, for establishment of pride of place. The Holy Roman Empire, which lasted for a while, even though some imagined at the time it was destined to last forever, can be seen as a heroic attempt to bridge the gap. It might have lasted longer, if the popes had concentrated on love and the kings on law but each became jealous of the other. The adoption of the Christian standard by Constantine's armies was a kind of beginning of a dovetailing effort but then we can notice how the glue did not hold, for example when we observe how Henry VIII loved and how celibacy became a Church law. Suffice it to say that the physiological separateness, the 'twoness', of intention and execution threw up problems of a nature both intimate and of far-reaching political consequence. If the nature of these problems was not recognized right away as physiological, as essentially rooted in contemporary, born human beings, this is hardly surprising. The physiology of the individual being is usually the last place where we look for causes and explanations for causes, especially if the nature of the case demands, that the individual be ourselves – me.

The nature of the present case demands just that. Power, especially purposeful power, is so tied up with individuality and personality, with the creative conscience of the single human being, albeit in community, that a merely academic, non-engaged approach to the topic is bound to court extinction from the outset. This, by the way, is how I would use that term 'extinction' – to describe non-purposeful performance, merely automatic, self- or ego-driven performance, or unintentional execution, where the inward realm is ignored or even resented and what should be outward, as a natural outpouring or outgrowth from the inward reality is instead outside, exterior and external – finally then extinct in the true sense of the word and quite the opposite of instinct.

I have no interest in playing off metaphysical against empirical preoccupations. It is how we view the 'twoness' of the person and the world, of myself and my environment, that happens to be so decisive for the theme in hand. If our purpose is limited to accidental, external data, if we intend nothing except contingencies as ends in themselves, such as happiness and loads of money all rolled into one, then we delude ourselves as effectively as that poor soul in the novel 'Rasselas' by Samuel Johnson, who held himself responsible for the weather of the globe, until he was cured by the kindly affection and infinite patience of those around him. Mystical contemplation and a reverence for matter should not be confused with mysticism and materialism. Kindly affection and infinite patience cure us of the latter and only then can we come to terms with that singular power which is to be gained and gifted due to the fact that purpose and intention are accessible separately from performance, from execution and any external reward.

*

2

The annoying discrepancy between what we wish we could do and what we come up with, puts us in mind of our weakness and perhaps even of our mortality. Right away we learn that only while we confess our weakness and mortality and make our peace with it, can we be endowed with the stuff that makes us strong and immortal. It makes sense, that while we insist on self-sufficiency and take pride in our independence from other sources, we are, at best, not open to increase from those sources. At worst, especially if it should turn out that potentially beneficial influence presses in upon us in any case from those other sources, we misinterpret this as disagreeable, harmful and even malevolent. Those whose understanding, whose science, is not extinct would vouch for it that, to use one possible terminology, God loves us whether we like it or not and rarely do human beings ignore that with impunity – or let us say: without incurring palpable disadvantage. The truth that this palpability is merciful cannot be more than indicated in the present context.

What we need to look at thoroughly is that in spite of, or along with, our realistic acknowledgement of our weakness and of the temptation to bluff our way in terms of force and forceful mechanisms, we carry within ourselves a perfectly sound desire for power. We admit we are weak and we wish to be powerful. On the surface this looks like a contradiction. A little deeper down it feels like a paradox. At bottom, however, it reveals itself as a perfectly rational state of being – and of affairs. Only to the extent that we confuse power with force and might, and weakness with inability and feebleness, do we have a problem with it.

Far be it from me to present this problem as readily solvable. We may instinctively understand what is wrong with us, even as we pursue the goals of extinction. It stresses us out abominably, that we cannot have recourse to a selective will-power and liberal choices without evidently and obviously distancing ourselves even more from a perceived source of comfort, health and strength. Truly we are to be pitied in that state.

We are pitied. I maintain that we are. In our smallness we may receive a variety of useful teachings. It is arrogance, not modesty or humility, that gets in the way of our real initiative. It gets in the way of our knowing what to do. Surely we wish to be useful and helpful to those around us, not a hindrance and a burden. This is a fundamental momentum of our humanity, the definitive urgency of our human being. Misdirected it occurs as dogmatic greed, as blinkered zealotry, as a thirst for might. Not misdirected we know it as power, which is the creative ability to do good.

It makes no sense to call it power, if no good comes out of it. Might is not creative but it inspires fear in proportion to its massiveness, which may not appear to leave us any choice. Might does not overcome anything but merely pushes what is less mighty out of the way. Political might forever operates on that level. We would call it silly, except for its tragic consequences and the absurd spectacle it presents. Power, by comparison, overcomes and since it is good by definition it overcomes evil. Evil evaporates in the presence of it. It does not humiliate its enemy but demonstrates how it can manage just as well without him. When we fear the loss of our enemies, we realize we cannot enjoy being mighty without them. United global culture and civilization cannot operate on a basis of might, no matter how sensitively balanced, – except temporarily again – if bad Martians were to turn up.

So much for that. If we agree on the definition of some of the concepts central to this discussion we can move on.

What has to be shown now is that true power, which is the creative ability to do good by overcoming evil, can only be initiated within ourselves and that it cannot be linked meaningfully, in its inception, to any external phenomena or forces. Evil arises in our hearts and makes its way out into the world, through our agency and neglect, unless we put a halt to it. It occurs to us as originally outside ourselves, only because we have not in time put a halt to it. In truth it originates in our hearts – in my heart. Here I am wise to anticipate the initial occurrence of it and to practice methods for dealing with it creatively, when it does occur. The terror in my heart is an evil which I can countenance intelligently. Why does it crop up? Why in me? Why now? The only reasonable answer to this always has to be: So that good may shine forth, in me, even now or as soon as possible. Woe to me if I let it out into my environment, this terror, there to become my enemy! The terrorist is much more difficult for me to countenance, especially to the extent that I refuse to admit my responsibility for his existence in the first place. All the same, he too will yield if in spite of my error I opt for power and not for might. I may not be able to change his mind but I can 'be' in such a way that he cannot harm me, while he may possibly even turn and help me.

How can I put a halt to the evil that arises in my heart, as envy, say, or fear, or greed? If I have opened myself to the suggestion, that evil does indeed arise and originate in my heart, I am bound to ask: What can I do to put a halt to it? How can I put a stop to it?

As a matter of fact I am not very likely to admit in the first place that evil stems from my heart, unless I have at least an inkling of how I might powerfully handle it. In my untutored ignorance, I will barely hesitate to blame all evil on those around me, on the weather, on the government, on the white or the black man, on the Moslem, the Jew or the Christian.

116

There, at least, I feel I have a chance to exercise my mighty right by resisting that evil, by destroying my enemy, by protecting myself with all the corporate aid of those I can persuade – or bribe, or threaten – to agree with me. I may become so addicted to this nonsense, that only the merciful shock of calamity or catastrophe will cause me to reflect and to reroute my thought and feeling.

What will really persuade me to adopt an inkling of trust and insight is some example of power in action. How many times do I have to see what happens when someone loves his enemy, before I am swayed to try my hand at it? Probably only the once. And in the neighbourhood of someone who manages to stop the evil that has originated in his heart, I am strangely moved to admiration – and to imitation. Not that I can be good. No one can 'be' good. But we can do good if we put our minds to it. First we have to face a few facts about ourselves, which are only superficially unpleasant.

Then we must intend to do good. It must be our purpose to do good. By this we must understand first of all the overcoming of evil in ourselves as it arises daily. An effective human being greets the evil on his inward path with a royal salute. He does not cringe, hoping for eternal convenience but welcomes the challenge as an opportunity for greater power. Why does he want more power? Why does he desire to be more creative? Because that is how he is fashioned. That is how a human being is originally created, with this inborn, human natural motivation to be helpful to the chap next to him in the bus queue, to be useful to the members of his community, to be of benefit to his natural environment, to the world at large and all beings in it, – human, animal, vegetal, etc.

Who in his right mind would want it otherwise?

*

3

Once the initial intention to do good is in place, particular opportunities soon present themselves. As soon as I 'purpose' to be powerful, I discover occasion to exercise that power, both within and without myself. It may take a while for the intention to stick and for the purpose to be genuine. It depends a lot on how long we have been away from it, from any down-to-earth investment of our original human nature.

The long-range effect of every powerful intention is as certain as it is incalculable. What I do with a genuinely good purpose in mind, does me as much good as anyone else but this must, initially at least, be a matter of belief. However belief is not mere belief, is not supposition or guesswork, until evidential experience should sweep over us and eradicate all doubt. Belief and faith are summoned up in ourselves, because we take the time to realize that this faculty is the mainstay of our personhood and as fundamental to all our other faculties as it is necessary for our daily existence, if we are not to succumb to stress and decay.

What is a genuinely good purpose? First of all it is something we hold and keep in mind, something we own. Let us not ignore the inspirational aspect of it. Good spirit influences us and if we are ready and willing and perhaps even welcoming, it deposits in us a genuine purpose. We carry that around with us for a while. That concentrates our attention and quickens our step. It may be a plan for cheering up our wife on mothers' day. It may lead to a decision to set up a charity in aid of flu victims. Those would be outward effects. It may also amount to a new organ of compassion. We may suddenly be fired with the notion, that a certain type of meditation makes us more receptive, more sympathetic, more capable of a new kind of foresight or hindsight, less quick to fly into a passion. Such a purpose is primarily concentrated in myself but being powerful, it cannot fail to radiate outward. All such inward purposes are fundamental and any statue erected on any other basis, no matter how altruistic-seeming, will topple or be toppled.

Purpose gathers whatever is available of value in ourselves and concentrates it towards some end. Beyond that end there are always, then, other ends and the process is ultimately endless. A 'sense' of purpose is nice but can be dangerous, depending on the magnitude of our sensual nature. We can get so carried away by our sense of purpose, that practical reason flies out the window and rational good and common sense is wasted, as compulsive self-abuse and morbid sentimentality. That way the power seeps out of the purpose, action becomes hectic or lassitude sets in. We can take ourselves to task, then, and resource the power through disciplined and even tactical prayer, for example. We do not have to wait for being shown up in public as fools or for being convicted in our private selves of impotence and lack of direction. Motivation itself has to be checked out before we leap on its back and gallop off. An honest examination of why we will do what we propose to do, may have to involve an exclusively inward courage and self-conquest, for which no glittering prizes are handed out. Before we can reconnect to our original and powerful intention, we may have to walk for a spell in the desert but why would we despair, if we have learned that this is how rescue works and how progress has to be managed at times? Help is always available. We ask for it and we have it already, since we opened our eyes and ears a little wider.

Genuine, powerful purpose requires no check. It compares to a patient co-operation by us with our soul. The inward glow of a knowledge, that has accumulated a drop at a time due to persistent enterprise and intelligent suffering, supplies warmth and light, so that whatever we undertake cannot but thrive. The very atmosphere in which our project flourishes is supplied due to that same solidarity with merciful good spirit within us which guarantees the initial conception of that project. We are never alone in what we do well, only in what we mess up. We need never be alone during the course of expiation, restitution or repair. Or, to put it another way, whatever helps us to be charitable towards others and disciplined in ourselves is a good thing.

*

4

My aim was to show how the power of purpose is essential to our human natural welfare and how, if properly conceived, this notion can pay worthwhile dividends. The drugs we abuse to dull our sense of self-defeat and the obsessions we entertain to cheat our way into states of euphoria, have this in common, that they signal our ignorance of the true source of power and of how far even intention on its own can get us. Of course we may be so busy masking our supposed social unacceptability, that even when the remedy stares us in the face, we brush it aside, because it reminds us of our deficiency.

Personal initiative seems to be a rare commodity. We cannot implant it in anyone by force of argument. All we can force, perhaps, is temporary activity based on fear but where fear operates, personality is surrendered. We cannot bring it out in anyone by means of punishment. Ordinarily punishment, if appropriate and just, may bring about reflection during a pause along the erroneous road, but personal initiative, powerful and purposeful, is a gift, which has to be courteously offered and gracefully accepted. Those in the know can demonstrate it. They can set the example, perfectly content in the knowledge, that this is the best they can do and that it may be a great deal. Meekness and mildness is more powerful and gets us further than self-assertion and self-advertising. One reason for this is that it can never be popular. "When they praise you," said a wise man, "quickly find out where you went wrong."

*

5

It is remarkable, how we can become empowered by a purpose, especially by a common purpose. I recall with pleasure the time when several of the parents of our integrated school in Northern Ireland joined up to construct the first straw bale house on the island. It was a modest affair, a single space of thirty square metres, with load-bearing walls and three windows at the rounded end. None of us were trained craftsmen or -women. We used common sense and the advice of someone who had built one before. That rare and singular reality of a community spirit soon came into evidence. We were companionable and enthusiastic about the task we had set ourselves. I noticed how some individuals, who were not otherwise noted for being particularly conscientious, were eager to do their best. Charitable allowances were made spontaneously for those who were less skilful. If something went wrong, such as when the wall bulged at the corner, the blame was readily shared. At the same time, there was plenty of scope for those who were hungry for work.

Projects like that succeed because the purpose is useful, simple and clear. No one was in it for the prestige, for money or for health reasons but purely to achieve a much-needed addition to the school's work space. Eventually, when the job was done, the television cameras did come around, some money was donated and probably we all felt healthier but those results, or rewards, had not been items on our agenda.

Looking back on that experience, I come to the conclusion that in the main, two things are important. First, of course, the purpose has to be clearly mapped out, not just in material terms but, perhaps more to the point, with a view to establishing sound and sane reasons for the task. Motivations have to be examined. If our purpose is selfish, the exercise will defeat us and any apparent reward is delusory. If we allow ourselves to be driven, we will end up fatigued. If we do what we do merely because we were told to do it, our actual purpose may well be to mask a lack of interest or to flatter a despot, which makes for no real gain.

Second, I Come back to my definition of power. For my own personal satisfaction I would always insist that real power is an ability to do good. Such power is personal and human and an interesting aspect of it has to do with the way it grows out of action and activity. In other words we do not need to wait until we have some evidence of being sufficiently powerful before we agree, or set out, to perform some purposeful action. A cheerful participation in such action, or even some solitary initiative, empowers us; It makes us powerful and leaves us with a greater capacity for doing good. This is what I mean when I say that purpose empowers us. A clear practical purpose empowers us clearly and practically.

It is important to know that and to have it ready to mind at such times as when fortune is against us and we seem to have nothing to give. We question our store of available resources, discover a scarcity and then arrive at the wrong conclusion: I am weak, therefore I cannot do. Instead I should be saying: I feel unable, impotent, etc., therefore I shall now do. The popular mistake is, to think that we need energy before we can put our hand or brain to something. What we need is a purpose. And, come to think of it, what better purpose, under the circumstances, than that we would like to be powerful, able and competent, rather than impotent, downcast and dismayed.

It is a mistake to suppose that we need energy before we can do. Out of that mistake arises the confusion of energy with power and of power with might. More or less energy put into some pursuit does not make it better or worse, just more or less energetic. The end result may be equally good, bad or indifferent, and all of these attributes would then apply to an effect, not to a work, as in the case of power. Might, by comparison, is availability and accessibility of energy. A mighty nation has ample weaponry but may be powerless, if those at the helm are not in touch with their human nature, so that all their aims will be contingent effects and their purposes can do no good. Political power is therefore a misnomer. The body politic can only be more or less effective, and always then in terms of some contingency.

Strictly speaking, if this expression 'the power of purpose' is to have meaning, we have to understand it in the context of good that is aimed at and pursued and we pretty well have to believe, not just to know, that our most fundamental and central – our human natural – desire is in fact to do good, under whatever circumstances. The sense of purpose involves our thinking, our deliberating and weighing of consequences, but never beyond the scope of strong and powerful motives. To the extent that force, energy and might come into it, power is depleted and good work is diminished.

A great deal therefore depends on the purpose I set myself. If I want to impress the world, beat the competition into the ground, aggrandize myself in the name of popular values, get a job done as fast as possible to be home for the football match, my purpose is not good and cannot result in power. If, on the other hand, my purpose is greater clarity, deeper insight, more fidelity in friendship and marriage, an honourable approach to certain public bodies or even just plain a way out of impotence and defeat, out of debilitating depression or arrogant high spirits, then these are powerful purposes in themselves and in good time power, or more power, will accrue to me.

Finally then, when we speak of the 'power of purpose' we imply good purpose, since a bad or indifferent purpose drains power and substitutes might, force and selfish satisfaction. At a time in history when criticism and a morbid curiosity about evil is culturally fashionable, force and might will impress, while purpose may well be called good but will not in fact be so. We will not even be able to come up with any good purposes, while we are wedded to a downward spiral and while we misuse language to delude ourselves into thinking that everything about us is wonderful.

Our human nature, however deeply we allow it to descend into misery or rise into the unconscionable void, contains within it an inalienable and secret store of creativity. This is never so completely overlaid with the rubble resulting from thoughtless and unfeeling business, that it cannot be unearthed and put to use in the light of day. Is it our purpose to forgive? To be merciful and compassionate? To understand rather than to overbear? To trust in providence rather than to act in fear? To celebrate good will in one another and practice gratitude in ourselves? To praise rather than to criticize? To respect our environment and learn a reverential approach to our natural habitat?

All this is available within our reach, in solitude or companionship. That is good to know, surely. And when we set ourselves the purpose to realize and actualize even one or two of such aims, we become more integrated and rooted within ourselves and then, when evil comes into our world, which it will sooner or later, we will not be swept off our feet and dragged along with the rest to destruction but our foothold will be secure. Far from fleeing from evil or resisting it, we will be able to transform it, creatively, to bring it into comparison with some victory of the good, and that is what it means to be powerful, and to be empowered.

* * * * *

Verse and Poetry

(a short comparison from
a practitioner's point of view)

In poetry the heart of man transcends,
in verse we but describe how this life ends.

To each its own task has been set
and each can do what it does best:
verse unifies the heart of man,
the poet sets it in our breast.

Versification of this and that
brings it within the sphere of sense.
The poet starts with real sensation
and overcomes the world's pretence.

Make a verse, make a rhyme,
fit yourself into space and time,
work freedom, create meaning.
The poem you become – you are –
leaves language-traces of its being
for communal hearing and seeing.

*

From the practitioner's point of view it would appear advisable to draw attention to a worthwhile difference and distinction that can be made, if one so chooses, between verse and poetry, and between versification and poetry. The purpose for this is not to give aid to the tedious process of describing, according to yet another system of classification, such poetry and verse as exist in the world, as if one could get more from a piece of creative work if one enjoyed it under one name rather than another. Wordsworth's "I Wandered Lonely as a Cloud" gains not much new appreciation, so far as I can see, from submission to fresh categories. But whether it does or not, I would urge a judgment on the score of 'verse and poetry' first and foremost for the sake of the new work that we all look forward to, such as the embodiment of a personal reality and the habituation of human qualities and values.

We are, understandably, on the look-out for new tools. A new reality seems to be opening up for us and we lack the instruments for dealing with it. Consequently we are often overwhelmed, stunned or perplexed. My suggestion of a new look at poetry as distinct from verse addresses itself therefore to this need for tools; in fact it arises out of an experience of this contemporary reality itself. Just as a poet once said that the sun calls forth the in living beings the visual organ of the eye, so I would argue that contemporary reality is ready to show us, if we attend, what particular tools are most suitable if we desire to live and worship in reality.

Now it happens that most of our concepts are outdated. These concepts were tools for dealing with something else. Take such concepts as will, intellect, consciousness; such as body and mind. There is a shift in emphasis, an inversion of meaning, and for a time these words clatter in us like so many rusty nails in a tin pot. Perhaps we ourselves are meanwhile being 'reborn' to become real. When next we seek to express ourselves we may for a while speak in tongues, as it were, with or without an interpreter, but eventually we will see wisdom in the faculty of understanding for the purpose of communication, and so we practically recreate language itself, word by word, and every concept is then different and new. Every creative person tries to accustom his nature to the experience of being misunderstood so that it will not hold him back as he yet again expresses what he knows first hand to be the case to those who have had to reject their own tools as useless but take them up again under the duress of contemporary reality in any guise.

The employment of the concepts 'body' and 'mind' is a good case in point. The old style usage raises mind above body somehow because body decays and mind is immortal, roughly speaking. Gradually, over a period of years, 'body' comes into a new usage until it stands beside 'mind' as an equal partner. A confusion sets in, the traditional one perhaps between 'seeming' and 'being', until one is willing to admit that 'in truth' the difference between body and mind is negligible. The two are conceived as one and this feels quite right and proper. The term 'flesh', or 'appearances' takes over to depict that which is given over to corruption, leaving body and mind inviolate as the two sides of the same coin. Lastly the difference, precisely, between these two sides is appreciated as significant and finally even structured and shaped, as men realize for themselves a new set of tools. 'Body' takes account of sense, of knowledge and of feeling while 'mind' little by little takes on currency as signal, sign and gesture, not as that which reflects and thinks but which is reflected and thought.

'Verse' and 'poetry' must also undergo such an inversion of meaning, and unavoidably this will happen under protest. We are either bowled over by these changes or we collaborate in their instigation and co-operate in their institution. We have the choice to be creative, or we cling to a worn-out world and go down with it.

Anyone can write verse. It comes readily to the pen. All you need is an opinion, an observation, a feeling or a mood and then lines compose themselves as if by magic.

For example:

> Anyone can write verse.
> It comes readily to the pen.
> All you need is an opinion, an observation,
> a feeling or a mood and then
>
> lines compose themselves as if by magic.

A good case could be made, and no doubt has been made, for a language itself consisting of verse and all it takes is for someone to speak that language well. But of course for someone to speak or write a language well he must be someone. He must be someone at the time of speaking or writing.

So anyone who is someone can write verse. The fact that a few of us actually do it is good because it advertises the sheer pleasure and the downright benefits of being someone, rather than being just something or – horrible to contemplate – not being at all.

The question of how we get to the point of actually being someone, someone with a heart and a head, with a will and an identity, this cannot have much to do with verse. A great deal that is made up and given out as verse amounts to no more than an incidental confession of not being anyone, of not yet being born into the state of man. The state of man can be a perilous state, so a lot of so-called verse seems for all the world to serve in the cause of the avoidance of that future peril. A voice is heard, but it's a blind voice, a deaf and dumb voice. It's a bad tree on which grows only bad fruit. Technically it's not a voice at all but a noise. Things by themselves make noise. The human being is lacking, and the person.

I sometimes suspect that only we as people can make this horrible noise, because nothing else I know of is at liberty to divest itself of all human being – of being as such. A brook has a voice. So does the wind, through the trees or across the corn. Birds, all animals in their own environment have voices.

But listen to the anxious whining and incessant yapping of a domesticated dog. What a pitiful noise is made by a stream of water out of a tap. We have just about succeeded in denaturing our environment. I limit myself to a small portion of it, to natural voice and unnatural noise. Go to an airport. The slick noises inside the buildings, the noises made by tortured metal outside, by natural energy on the rack! Why do people denature their environment? To suit it to themselves, it's as simple as that.

We degrade our environment down to our own level. It begins with ourselves. The human nature goes out of us and we don't prevent the regression. We disperse our humanity and dispense with it, for the sake of a little popularity and prestige or from sheer laziness. If we don't gather, we scatter. Verse can be looked at as a gathering activity, as a gathering in this sense of nature and human nature, and in the direction of human being for the purpose, ultimately, of a lively personality. So verse does have an ethic tendency. It runs contrary to self-indulgence and by means of it we can come to appreciate our existence more successfully because we do exist to that extent for others. The most modest versification is such an existence for others:

> You know that I may not exactly
> like you for how you appeal to me
> but think of the joy it gives me
> to have you here in my company.

> Elsewhere who knows how you fare,
> perhaps not at all understood by
> those who like you and please you,
> left in the lurch by them
> when an insult can be construed,
> or made to face the music by yourself
> when precisely there is no music.

> Even now in your absence
> I endeavour to make room for you,
> in my heart and in my mind too,
> so that a practical solution may
> eventually be discovered by us
> for the problem of our dispersion.

When we write verse we can only get the best out of this medium by setting ourselves very definite limits. When, during the course of versification, we come to the end of those set limits we must ask ourselves, do we want to continue to write verse or not. If we do, then we have to limit ourselves anew, right then and there, on the spot.

Now this current and contemporary limitation is in fact what gives verse its high interest and effectiveness. What counts is that it is we ourselves, I myself, who set the limits and who set them for the distinct purpose of an on-going versification.

What kind of limits are they? Simply the limits of my own acknowledged individuality. Each time when I say: 'I am individual', or 'I am individual in this or that way', I discipline my spirit, and I do it, obviously, for your sake and for the sake of others, since no one can discipline his spirit for his own sake. No one writes verse so as to burn it or speaks verse principally for his own benefit.

An Encounter

We have nothing in common with each other.
You worship the ground that you stand on,
in it you will eventually be buried
and no one will remember you except
perhaps your dog, for a day.

We have nothing in common. Our eyesight
stretches in opposite directions so that
what you call an end, or a horizon,
for me becomes an element of achievement,
not even acknowledged as such.

And yet I seek you out for an hour
to lend an unbiased ear to your criticisms

because in you I see myself, externalized.
By overcoming my reaction to your treacheries
I make room for the tolerance of my own.

*

Writing verse is serious business. What I mean is that we can achieve something by writing verse. We can, for example, achieve clarity, such as in the above.

Again, the individuality of the writer circumscribes every word and every line. I speak of the writer rather than of myself, because of the change in myself since then, due to that achievement of clarity. It would seem appropriate at the moment to highlight that change, lest we mistake our individuality for a law or for a state.

This openness to change accounts for the dynamics of verse. As soon as I set myself the task of the versification of something I endeavour to keep in mind and to remain aware as constantly as possible of the changing nature or being of my object. If my own individuality is my object, as in the previous verse, I have it easy, because I have to remain open and nothing else. Call it a metaphysical openness. If I versify something other than my individuality, I have the additional problem of a closure out there. Metaphysical verse is distinctive because of its immediate comprehensibility, but then again this very immediacy puts some of us off and we prefer the roundabout way of coming to grips with things:

> The test of what you are
> is your prospective annihilation.
> How do you respond to that?
> Can something be done
> to assure you of our gratitude?

> When the world forecloses on you
> have you something to fall back on?

When the silence absorbs you
and god has moved behind the mountain
do you hold still for the duration

or do you flail about in your psyche,
a nuisance to god's other children?
Your annihilation is only proper,
why make a fuss about it?
Who else would demonstrate the resurrection?

*

What is being versified here? The overcoming of self-annihilation, or the conquest of the defeated self. The experience of impotence is identified and recognized. It is utilized as a relevant limitation or boundary to the creative act.

A verse is a trace or record of something that has been done. It also is evidence of how this was accomplished, and in such a way that someone else can accomplish it for himself, though much more readily. By writing verses we clear paths and build bridges for others:

There where you look now,
your eye espoused to the light of day,
a million angels lead you to your destiny,
so sit down and make yourself comfortable.

You have aroused the ire of the elements,
of powers and principalities,
by your annexation of new heart-room
                        and head-space
so please confirm your choices.

Be comforted now
by the one who teaches you all things,
so that tomorrow will be a day for you
and not a senseless prolongation of ill will.

*

The versification of something – certainly not of someone: what is it that is being accomplished? Why do we versify – a mood, an event, something that has made an impression on us? Do we try to raise it to a higher level of awareness? Do we try to become aware of it at all, being only conscious of it?

We mentioned an achievement of clarity. There is the necessity of remaining within intentional, contemporary limits. We also observed that we can either decide on limits we set ourselves or else adopt something as a boundary which would otherwise be a constraint or even something we resist. We don't resist the limitation we choose. We can pick up our cross and carry it gladly rather than being depressed by it.

Choosing the limitations of our individuality : this is surely a step, the classic step, towards freedom. The fact that I am someone in particular here and now, rather than merely a specimen or an example; rather than merely a member of a group or a biological accident – this is what my individuality means. There is a point beyond which I cannot be divided any further. I think that's one thing we mean to get at when we speak of our individuality. It's important to many of us. We are liable to insist on it; which I don't recommend, by the way; we sacrifice our personality in that way. But that's another story, and it touches on the crucial question of individual rights. Usually what happens, the way I see it, is that when I insist on my own individuality I also abuse yours. There is probably no way around that.

When I notice how much importance this business of an individuality is assuming here in connection with the act of versification I feel inclined to place this act among those by which we keep our individuality in perspective and in harness. Let's see what happens if we approach the next verse from that angle:

I assume I have waited long enough
when the light begins to seep in between
myself and my perception of myself.
In that light I recognize your face
which pleases me immensely because
now I can forget about my self
and concentrate on living.

My self is like
an apple core stuck in my throat,
so that I choke on my self
and the world turns upside down.

I would much rather
behave like a fool in public
than quietly crawl into a corner and die,
but the truth of the matter is
that until you appear on the scene,
utterly at peace with yourself
and totally forgiving,
I am a burden and a pain.

So I close my eyes and wait.
In hell they don't like to be disturbed
so I keep my thoughts to myself
and proceed on light feet.
I do this work because I want to do it,
I try to keep that in mind,
but in cases like the present,
when the sickle-man dogs my steps
and in front of me all is dark,
I cast my net no further than would seem
appropriate under a lack of circumstances.

Still there is pressure in the region of the heart,
the diaphragm feels impeded, the head
like lead, or like a furnace burnt out.

Suddenly no concepts are available
and I merely lean into the wind
without shrinking from the fire.

As soon as the medication reaches the brain
there is momentary release from self
and one hopes to utilize, to best advantage,
one's liberty, to turn it into freedom.

*

Liberty turned to freedom : that strikes me at the moment as
an apt definition of versification in terms of the active human
being. Certainly creativity may be there when we need it, but
the more mature adult surely would consider it a point of honour not to wait for a surfeit of circumstances before exercising
his human prerogative. No, he would seek out creative opportunities especially when there is no need and when he is at liberty, at liberty to do and to behave as he would, since only
then can his authenticity come fully into play, when his nature
is not compromised by other natures and when he is under no
obligation to aspects of his environment.

Qualities of human being that I associate with liberty are sobriety, ease, a readiness to act and a receptivity to the extra-
individual or strange. I think of the last two as of equal importance with the first two. In the absence of them our liberty is
even then at risk because the sobriety and the ease have become
self-indulgent for us, and we in them. On the other hand we
cannot enjoy sobriety and ease unless we have decided on a certain attitude or stance vis-à-vis our problems, pains and psychic
states in general. We touched on this earlier. We mentioned
how an uncomfortable condition by which we are constrained
can be chosen, or adopted, by us as a profitable limitation for
the purpose of creative progress such as in terms of versification. The underlying faith of course will be that pain is meaningful, that it makes sense, whether we see the meaning and

know the sense at that moment or not. In the absence of fundamental faith, these considerations cannot possibly appeal.

I would argue then that we do well, as practitioners, to understand creative verse as arising out of our self-conditioned
human liberty; at a time, in other words, when we have accepted
and assented to all constraints on our individuality for the time
being, understanding them in faith as essentially and potentially
productive. Verse becomes truly rich and effective when we can
manage to turn the tables like this on the so-called demons and
elements that beset us again and again, as soon as we are considered sufficiently worthy and capable to deal with them:

> Overreach yourself only one inch
> and the clouds tumble down on you,
> crash into you, destroy you.

> But once destroyed, you still stand open-eyed,
> though the hand is shaking,
> and you traverse to a new level,
> to an alpine meadow above the foothills,
> there to disport yourself.

> What can they finally do to you,
> the messengers of fear and worthlessness?
> Can they bring you to your knees?

> Yes they can, and they have done.
> But then you rise up, refurbished.
> Can they remove from the eye and from the ear
> the world's glad face and sweet enchantments?
> Nothing more normal in the way of things,
> even as if it delighted them,
> because then, don't you see, they expect –
> nay, they have a right to expect –
> blame laid and perversity indulged,
> since after all you were attached to these.

But only ask for love and there she stands,
dewy-eyed love, perplexed by your audacity,
or the love that holds firm within misery
once the gate has clanged shut
and the bolt has slid into position.

And then downright reality reveals itself
as utter imagination. It occurs with such
speed! You have neither
time nor willingness to reflect, as if
the cosmos had enlarged to needlepoint,
there to unfold its attractions.

The universal talent tends to blindness
and must be daily recharged
else humility is lost
and the strength that should be ours
flaps in the wind.

And the wind whines its sad tale daily
through the chinks of your armour,
or breezes transport glad tidings
from far off where you wish you felt love
to once again clothe the shivering soul.

*

Implicit in this is the other meaning that I would like to see
in my own individuality, namely my inward divisibility. I
don't believe that one has to stretch the word too far to make it
do valuable service in this light.

My individuality implies that I am inwardly divisible. I am
not only divisible in two, or in four, but endlessly and completely divisible.

In that sense I think of myself not as a soul but I imagine
myself as spirit. I don't see why it should be wrong of me to
do so. When I think of myself as spirit I place myself entirely

in the hands of objective and subjective reality. Then when I try to point to myself, even for my own edification or amusement, I cannot find myself. I am utterly divided. There is a fusion of myself with the spirit that is sometimes called god. It may begin very gradually, this fusion, and at times I imagine I can see it coming from a long way off. There is a clinging to appearances and a rebellion against dissolution, but deep down I know that I am a problem presently being solved.

The division may start as a duality of myself and the world, so that I am not any more at peace with the world but strife has set in to remove me from it. There is myself and there are all others. What is wrong with me? What is wrong with the world? In either case a further division takes place, more inward, of myself into an observer and a process, of myself into a person and a self. Then my self divides, becoming ego and psyche, my person becomes public and private; the observer I am becomes the observer I was and the one I will be while the process of myself as I experience it becomes both sensible and mysterious. On and on goes the division until I become quite transparent and invisible, not only to myself but to others also. They speak to me but know they really speak to themselves. They blame me but I know they blame themselves, and the same with their praise.

The important achievement for me personally in this respect is that I call this individuality good; that I do not fight this on-going divisibility of myself but that I learn to trust it as the diastole, so to speak, of life. Life as systole and diastole. As I gradually come apart inwardly into smaller and smaller units I become as it were a vacuum that cannot help but draw into itself whatever presently exists. Life is greater than I. I live therefore as one in sorrow from whom all things part, like in Rilke's Elegy: angels, men and the canny beasts. The diastole of life. I distinctly dissolve and I know, or at least I hope I remain aware of the fact, that this negative individuality is as much of a marvel as the positive, contracting individuality is a mystery. What if I were to reject one or the other? What if I were to construct a system in the name of positive achievement for the purpose of denying the negative resignation?

> Systole and diastole of the heart.
> We give in to life and we give our life.
> We take hold and we let go.
> There is verse and there is poetry.

*

> The sun's warmth on the brown wall
> for a moment, while I thought of you
> and then stale memory for a year.

*

There is no reason why I should not describe much more intimately this obverse side of my individuality which amounts to an inward division.

We can probably say that vision is common to both. Vision informs us of our soul as body. Sight, hearing, feeling, all the senses depend on vision. But we can actually 'envision' something. We can become one with it through vision. Beatific vision for example means physical union with god.

Just as we can give in to life and give of our life, so can we 'envision' ourselves, specifically, or the one who is not ourself. We could not say that we envision a thing, because vision is always personal and of one.

Our individuality, both face and obverse, is really a product of our vision, either of vision outward or of vision inward. Vision and individuality go together.

The individuality on which poetry draws goes along with inward vision. What we envision can become the stuff of poetry. What we envision entrusts itself to us in the ripeness of time.

139

Again there is the phenomenon of making room, of getting a place ready, which will then be visited by the one whose coming is known, but not ahead of time by us.

The face side lends itself to verse. The obverse side lends itself to poetry. The obverse side is individuality as dissolution, as resignation, as a dividing up of oneself.

And to what end?

When we concerned ourselves with verse and with versification, we mentioned freedom as the goal. Now, in the case of poetry, there is every indication that the end is love. We can make room in ourselves for someone or even for something for the purpose of fondness and affection but when we ourselves, individually, efface ourselves and get out of the way for the other one, that betokens love.

We could say, therefore, that reality testifies to the poet's love and the poet delivers up to us that testimony.

We might, for our present purpose, distinguish between the poet and the bard, where the latter is responsible for verse while the former gives us poetry. The emphasis is in fact on responsibility in the case of verse, and on the gift where the poet is concerned. The bard may address himself to whatever he likes and he must do so responsibly, that is to say with regard to personal veracity and genuine authenticity. The poet, by comparison, passes on the gift of reality. He is primarily a lover, and the gift he passes on to us will in turn persuade us, and possibly even enable us, to love. Reality as given is his proper domain. In order to experience 'the other one' as given, rather than as achieved, he must first of all show himself as capable of love and then he must exercise, practice and demonstrate that love. His individuality will be, in his case, entirely at the service of that which is greater than his individuality and which allows itself to be called reality or the spirit that is god.

The one I hold in high esteem
must wait for me until I move
and quite remove myself from these
enchantments of the working mind
which entertain but will not please.

The one I hold in high regard
sees fit to keep me to my task
while all around me values break
to be replaced by gifts of love
engendered here for mankind's sake.

The one I would not do without
to save myself from any pain
or hindrance to the virile flesh
brings such constraint to bear on me
as must eventually refresh.

The one who lifts me into love
when all my steps have been dispersed
makes life out to be wondrous clear
among the god-forsaken ruins
deposited by history here.

The one whose magnitude and grace
enlivens what we are and do
beyond the calculating brain
and quite outside the range of sex,
prefers that I do not complain.

But daily I remove my gaze
from what my mind would reproduce
as though it knew the ins and outs
and by-ways of creation's scheme,
of its own self the whereabouts.

Then happy and effective care
informs the way I live and love,

all wisely laid out and arranged
as pattern simple to behold
and never from itself estranged.

Outrageous rationale of force
predicts its imminent demise
but caters to historic change
as if each hour were jet-propelled
through space within existence-range.

Or blatant logic digs its spurs
into some hobby-horse's flanks
and scrambles through the sinful night
past monstrous aberrations whose
enticements would impair our sight.

So technical have we become
within our torture house of science
that some would say we rush bereft
of sense throughout sensation's sphere
until no speck of truth is left.

*

It's a beguiling notion, that poetry should appear as soon as
the poet removes himself from the scene to make room for the
gift of reality. And it does sound easy. But the life of the poet
is one of being continually exposed to the elements of human
nature. The one who creates sanctuary for so many is not allowed sanctuary himself – not if he wants to continue to be a
poet. So by the time he gets around to the act of poetry itself,
the main part of his work is done. He has acquiesced to the
fact that his individuality is to be burdened so that eventually it
can dissolve into poetry. He carries that burden where he is
and where he goes, even as it accumulates. The great poet can
carry a great burden because the truth for him is personal. The
minor poet tries to carry the burden himself so the truth cannot
be revealed to him and he largely reflects it. His nature is oth-

erwise predisposed. Nevertheless he will be in earnest and persuaded by the importance of his task. The major poet shares
his burden with other poets. The communal element takes root
in him and he works towards a tradition. But the great poet
stands alone in the sense that his burden is of all humanity,
which he can only shoulder if he is open to the spirit of humanity, (which is also the spirit of truth in person) because the
effect of his spirit is the well-being of all men, women and
children:

> I long for the approval of my fellow man,
> that he should
> approve, indeed, of his spiritual heritage
> and not squander his substance.

> I would ask that a monument be set
> to the perpetrators of crimes,
> where those crimes have located for us
> new avenues for the pity of the underdog,
> for compassion in the realm of the psyche.

> Not all our benevolence is misguided,
> once we have realized in ourselves
> the extent of our capability
> for compassionate crime.

> Truth can announce itself
> at the drop of a hat
> for dissident exploration.

> The children have been brought up to respect
> every inch of territory laid waste by their elders
> and you would counsel against crime?

> But I tell you that the criminal in our midst
> favours the sun like yourself
> but does not necessarily
> make use of it to burn

the face of his brother.
Therefore tolerate the criminal in your midst.

Not the murderer, not even the thief,
but the criminal,
whose nature must exploit the falsehood there
as if he himself were responsible for it,
and explore the falsehood here
as if the memory of it could destroy him.

But read between the lines.
We have nothing to gain from
a literal interpretation of what moves a man's heart,
so if a woman can do it,
the more power to her.

*

Verse and poetry combine finally to take the fullest possible advantage of a language as it is spoken. We recognize in the preceding work a movement from liberty to freedom and simultaneously with this we can trace the gift-content, which builds gradually to the revelation at the end. The depth of the work is not obvious. One can read from beginning to end without being struck by the tragic element inherent in the experience, but the stanzas, which should perhaps be called verse stanzas, do discourage a narrative and descriptive orientation. (The aphoristic verse-stanza.)

Finally we can try self-explanatory examples of all three: verse, poetry and verse poetry, (poetic verse?) to make more obvious what can be done in each case and what must be left to the spirit of reality.

*

Verse

A succinct compilation of words
rowed end to end

144

to manifest at once
the human heart at work
and the force of individuality –

You rack your brains but nothing comes,
which only demonstrates
to the marauder demon
how self-propulsion leaves the spirit cold.

Verse makes demands on your mettle.
You cannot pretend to be otherwise occupied.
Overlook one single complex of the psyche
and the passage is blocked,
fear reaps its reward.

Part of you pays heed to the
downright mysterious side-effects that wish to be
unobtrusively included, otherwise
there is padding, my friend,
and nothing changes.

You do no doubt wish to get on with it.
May your troubles be little ones.
Cultivate the masterful awareness
and take care not to resist evil.
Animals' may look in on you.

Outwardly you have nothing to complain of
since discipline has arranged matters
so as to render them subtle in the light.
But the calculations of meaning need
universal justification.

Therefore you may draw your conclusions
like a man who is satisfied
because his tears have cancelled out his laughter.

*

Poetry

By your leave,
I make this fascinating suggestion
but I do not expect praise.
A poem about poetry
lacks lustre in many ways
right from the start,
so attempt no work of art

but do comment on the weather.
The amazing thing is this,
that so many poets have left themselves
open to cruel body and wild mind
in their eagerness to please,
in their ambition to
tease from an experience or two

the rudiments of a collective sensation.
Then when the wild boar
leaps from covert,
tearing and shredding the psyche,
problematic life seems like a
ball in comparison.
Order and chaos must be

equal spheres of influence for the poet.
Are you not maybe
ready for a session with the shrink?
Perplexed, we emanate anxiety,
disastrous duties are laid on us,
spillages occur. You must know that
wherever the eye meets itself

there you make plans uselessly.
Deny yourself and follow me
said the arch poet, though he too could

turn a phrase to good advantage,
and the sheep will entrust themselves
to the shepherd who stays around
when your ego is on the prowl.

*

Verse poetry

My ego has its trial or trump
year in year out. The lump
in my throat, the castration complex,
the vivid fancies of sex, all these

leave me slightly dismayed when I
contemplate the living word.
I make too many grandiose plans
and that's a fact.

The wise decision
is to tackle the next inhibition
and the room with a view
will always include you.

This business can be put in
an infinite number of ways
and there lies the joy of it.
Propagation of political intrigue
has so much less to offer that I
turn continually away from
the machinations of my independent intellect
towards that girl striding past outside
in case I can return the compliment.

Or suddenly it becomes much more meaningful
to energize my environment
by carefully stepping back from it
and then I gradually learn the news from there.

Skills are worth learning,
like the right hand from the left hand in a
boxing match. Would you be
able – willing – reluctant – eager
to try something like this yourself?

* * * * *

What is a Priest?

So the word of god is an issue of many a concern where people are concerned, and we make some headway towards a notion of priesthood if we take into account the distinction of popular from human.

Not bread alone, but every word from the mouth of god: that is the issue here, for a priest can be said to be able to make himself accountable for every word of god.

Since god is spirit, the issue of this spirit, although mercifully manifold, cannot in itself be tied down to some particular manifestation, but must be left free, by us, to take shape where and however it pleases. Do we have a word, even a single concept, for all the possible and actual and probable and palpable manifestations and shapes of merciful good spirit? Are we wise to attempt such a thing? Or would we perhaps be smart to limit ourselves to the realm of the metaphoric in this case?

Speech, what we mean by speech, seems to me to be a fine and rather universal metaphor for that which issues from our father god. Speech itself could be called a gift of god, and then we compare all other gifts to this one, by describing them, or rather by referring to them, as words. There are as many genuine and useful ways of talking about this as there are competent human beings who take an interest and choose to make it their concern.

Spirit becomes flesh. As soon as I say that I realize I have put something into words that embraces, literally, everything. At the same time I note, rather gratefully if I may say so, that I am such a one as is able to do that, to put it into words, to say it. Do I not feel that something about me is special, that I should be able to make sense of this simple, universal thought? It makes me feel privileged and responsible. If someone walked up to me now and said: "If you are able to make such a thought – no, this particular thought – your own, you evidently have what it takes to point others in the direction of an exemplary life, and, let's face it, a certain onus is on you actually and really to do that, not just to talk about it. If you were to talk about it only, and not also act on your conviction, you would lower yourself from the status of a free human being to that of an inhibited functionary, and at the moment there are plenty of these around."

Ah, it sinks into my limbs like lead, such an appeal. I experience on the spot how the good spirit becomes not only flesh, but in this present instance my flesh. Why does that happen to me right now? I assume it is because in response to that appeal I have in fact expressed an intention to do exactly what the onus is, admittedly, on me to do. Even by saying to my interlocutor: "You are right," I have placed myself in a unique position in the face of god. I have physically allowed that I am willing to manifest the good spirit that is god as my flesh.

What does that mean for those around me? For you, for example?

I am not suggesting, by the way, that these notions I am putting forward are, in the particular, readily accessible to a modern mind. Such a mind would have to confess to itself its peculiar limitations if it were not to obstruct any degree of understanding of these notions. A modern mind will throw up its hands with equal facility in consternation or prayer, while the human heart goes hungry. With that note sounded, I continue.

*

Your flesh, and when you have something that you can, in truth, call your flesh, is that which makes you available to me, right here and now, in space and time. If it is your flesh, and not just dead matter that hangs on you and weighs you down, as some sort of modern envelope of your psyche – if it is in truth yours, this flesh, then that makes you yourself a manifestation of good spirit, and I congratulate you. We cannot do better on earth than to manifest good spirit. But before you rush to any conclusions, before you can call anything *your* flesh, your mind must be liberated from your body and your body from your mind, so that they can join in a working relationship. That comes first. Your hands must be untied and identified by you as left and right, so that you can use them. Your thinking and your feeling, if they are to be linked as works, such as real speech, for example, must first of all be cleansed, healed and taught. It has to be a sane mind and a sound body that get together, and it has to be a deliberate articulation, not an egotistic drive.

If all that holds good in your case now, then you will indeed be given the good to hold. You will know when the time has arrived. Until then you neither rest nor lay your head down, until you are free in body and mind. Don't worry if you are in prison or in hospital. That has to do with the flesh, which is not yet yours, and nothing in that department can seriously hold you back from your deliberations. Your mind and your body, as they become yours, are entirely under your individual jurisdiction. Of course if someone shows you a kindness out here, more power to you and to them. I mention all this about body and mind to indicate the system of priorities. I don't think anyone need concern himself overmuch about what it means to be a priest prior to an all around foundation of their individuality.

However, at the moment, when you are, as it were, clothed with your own flesh, you begin to make genuine, personal contributions to the welfare of your fellow men, women and children, and then the fun begins.

*

So your flesh is you as a manifestation of good spirit.

151

Now a priest is such a one as offers his flesh for the welfare of others.

Your flesh is what allows me to point and say: This is your flesh. If I can point at *you*, things are otherwise. He who supposes he can point at a priest is in error. We can see or hear a priest, but we cannot look at or listen to him. I hope this make sense to you. It has to do with the difference between mere appearances and real appearance. Every word counts.

Poetically now: If a priest sees you coming he knows what to do because all his instincts are alert to you as the one in need of sustenance and guidance. You see that priest and make yourself known to him as a one in need of sustenance and guidance. Then, if you both take advantage of the situation, which is not necessarily always the case, a transaction takes place. There is something you give to the priest, and there is something the priest gives to you. Both of you will know that this is going on, and you will confirm it. You both decide to behave in a particular fashion and you leave the success of your intention to the father who is merciful good spirit. Never suppose you can trade with a priest who is not aware of his merciful father, for such a one is a priest only in public or in private; only on show or in hiding, but not in truth and reality.

Philosophically: The priest we all know as the one who feeds and guides us is the Messiah or Christ. Not that the Messiah is a priest, but in him, among much else, does every priesthood reside. If I were a priest, I would naturally rely on the Messiah for sustenance and guidance, and I would pass these on to whoever applied to me for them. In that way I would be more myself, and those who applied to me could be more themselves. As a priest gives out substance and guidance, he himself is sustained and guided. The transaction is one of mutual honour and respect. Each recognizes himself in the other. As in the case of all human beings, there must be communion. The priestly transaction is not unique in this. Communion is the sharing of their life by human beings. What makes the priestly transaction unique is the presence of the Messianic in the flesh of the priest. This announces itself during the course of ordinary human communication. As we meet and greet one another, are we not wise to be open to all possibilities?

Scientifically: A priest makes no outward show of himself as a priest. No one can point to him and say truthfully: This is a priest. Neither does he make a secret of it, hoping to influence people through the power of the spirit without their knowing. He who identifies himself as a priest is not a priest. As soon as he makes that identification of himself he shuts the kingdom of god to others, and therefore also to himself. The priesthood is messianic and any priesthood is of the Messiah.

Priesthood is what you espouse if you make that transaction of meaningful humanity your particular business and personal domain. You do not espouse 'the' priesthood, but priesthood, which is not an idea but substantial reality. Anyone who espouses substantial reality (every word counts) does the father's secret work out here.

You will say: Ah, but once he espouses priesthood and once he is full time in human relations on that particular basis, surely we can point him out to one another and stick a label on him : priest! – Quite right, you can always do that, but as soon as you do, you spoil your chances of a messianic transaction by shutting the door to any further priestly influence. And if he goes so far out of his way as to acknowledge that label, he spoils his own chances. Remember that the worthwhile things fall to those who know what they do, not to those who are drawn this way and that by their inclinations and desires. Remember it well, what I tell you here, and guide your tongue. As many are identified in public as priests as bar the way.

For people must point to appearances, else they cannot live by them. But the popular life is no life at all. As many as congregate to pool their resources are deprived of their resources.

*

Popularity is espoused by those who are happily part of the world and not in the world. From the worldly or popular point of view god is a myth and his priests serve that myth. People belong to a tribe or club of one sort or another, and they like to see themselves as representatives of one thing or another. Thus the popular priest stands for something, for a set of attitudes, for example, and he clings to a group. People cannot stand alone because their individuality is not fit for personality. This in turn is so because they reject the Messiah. Popular priests sanction this rejection and trade on it. Massive feelings are taken for evidence of religion, while true religion is not entertained or aspired to.

What is the task of a true, messianic priest in the presence of people? How can he face the popular element and not condemn it? Is there still hope that the worldly will turn and open their eyes and see their salvation?

Certainly nothing can be achieved here by argument based on reason, since reason presupposes itself as a common basis or bond. No such bond exists between people and human beings. Shall we say with Paul of Tarsus: Would we could buy their salvation with ours? Or: When all the rest have seen, these too will see? The circumstances are hardly the same. And yet there is a common element of concern. It is simply the concern of those who are right for those who are wrong. And a priest will know he is on the right track if people give him neither pain nor pleasure, if they neither please him nor hurt him, while he goes about his business. And his business is the sustenance and guidance of those who come to him for sustenance and guidance. People neither accept him nor reject him, because they cannot possibly have any experience of him, since he cannot be known or identified by mere appearances, the popular criteria.

Where a priest manages to make his influence felt, this is of course appreciated by those who share with him the advantage. But if they know him, as by his works, they also know he is not to be identified in public or appealed to in private. Just as his messianic future was kept as a secret by Jesus, so as to avoid wrong expectations, so is his chosen priesthood kept as a secret by every real priest.

We are always in need of guidance and sustenance. Let us look for it and expect it from the person next to us. That alone suffices to bring it to the fore.

How does a priest face up to one who says he is a priest? As to all people. We take them as they are. And how are they? As we find them. There is no possibility of communion, while communication must remain superficial, on the level of appearances, which are mere for people and everything but mere for human beings. And therein lies the only hope for an exchange.

* * * * *

What it Means, to Know Oneself

The least bit of disagreement is liable to set off in us a disagreeable mood. Such a mood would put us in mind of our inner resources. Instead of taking advantage of this, we question the reason for the disturbance. We activate justification for the way we feel. Our usual sense of order no longer supports us. It's as if we were suddenly engaged, against our will, in a contest of forceful emotions, that draws our attention in terms of survival, of fight or flight.

It is a mighty contest in which we are liable to find ourselves. It is mighty inasmuch as good spirit is not involved and ethical values are not considered. What interests us about this contest is not so much that it can be set off by the least peccadillo, depending on our frame of mind, our condition of body or our state of soul, but rather what intrigues us here, in this present study, is how on one level we would like one side or the other to win, to come out on top, but on a higher level we would dearly like to be rid of what from that level looks to us like nothing but chaos. We might think, regretfully: However did I get caught up in this again! Give me peace. It really doesn't matter to me who is right and who wrong.

It's important, for what follows, to understand the nature of the predicament we find ourselves in. We can speak of two levels of mere existence, of non-being or not-yet-being, depending on how we proceed and on whether or not we proceed. We can get increasingly caught up in the struggle for survival until in one way or another we die. Every struggle for survival ends in death. Both those who are wrong and those who are right must die, since no good spirit is involved. If instead we search, in depth and in earnest, for a way out of the chaos and for a build-up of security that will make a future entrapment and confinement in chaos less likely, we draw on good spirit and eventually enjoy freedom. The search itself is a case of drawing on good spirit.

By knowing ourselves we draw on good spirit and remove ourselves from the merely existential chaos.

*

Not many of us will agree on what knowledge is and on what actually goes on when we know. Most will mean, by knowledge, something like information, external or internal descriptive facts, about this and that. What we have heard of is what we know.

Then there is knowing how to do one thing or another. We may know according to rules and regulations of knowing, such as arithmetic shows us.

The knowledge that overrides them all is an aspect of love and of loving. We definitely wish it well, what we know, however good spirit always wishes us well, so if I know you, not only does good spirit wish you well directly but also indirectly, through me, and this indirect love-knowledge is what interests us especially when we want to find out what if means to know oneself. Evidently it means to love oneself, in a knowing way.

If love unites us with what we love, then knowledge embodies for us what we know. Do we embody ourselves? Do we increase our body, our body of knowledge, when we know ourselves? What I embody is sensed, felt, impassioned.

How can I sense myself?

Well, I suppose first of all I have to be somebody. An individual, by definition does not know himself because he lacks the personal integrity. An individualist actually resists it, wants nothing to do with it. Good will, good spirit, diminishes, for him, his self-proclaimed status.

The intention to know himself however moves an individual into the realm of personality, where he lives for the other, or for another. So as soon as he knows himself he is no longer an individual but a person and his individuality is fluent and live.

So here we have one benefit of knowing ourselves, even intentionally, in that we become someone, a human being to be reckoned with.

As we continue to know ourselves, now and again, for sensible periods of time, we make ourselves more accessible to world and good spirit. We become more knowledgeable.

*

Now lets take a look at what else happens when we know ourselves. Of course we come up against ourselves as we are at that moment, it could not be otherwise. We come up against ourselves as <u>human and divine</u>, as <u>wicked and virtuous</u>, as <u>mortal and immortal</u>.

Here we get into the nitty-gritty of knowledge as action, specifically as creative action. To the degree that these pairs seem contradictory to us, we have our work cut out for us.

Let's look at the first pair, <u>our divinity and our humanity</u>. By dint of our birth we are human. Our nature is human. However due to the fact that good spirit influences us and that we open ourselves to this influence, we are divine. Do we have a problem with this? If so, this problem will reveal itself to us as soon as we know ourselves. We have a choice now, either to continue to know ourselves in order to solve this problem, creatively, or else to make the mistake of supposing that our knowing ourselves caused the problem, whereupon we cease to know ourselves.

Each of us will, of course, be faced with different problems, due to this revelatory effect of knowing ourselves. Since our continuing to know ourselves is necessarily creative, creativity implying an overcoming of hindrances to growth, there must also be a product. We will have something to impart. So our knowing of ourselves is productive of communal goods and commodities inasmuch as difficulties exist for us in accepting ourselves as both human and divine.

*

How silly it would be to suggest that in response to certain shortcomings in ourselves we might say: Ah yes, here once again I come across this inability in myself to harmonise my divinity and my humanity. No, in a research essay such as the present, what we look for are revelations of our actual being and also tools, faculties, that will provide us with a greater power of impact on the quality of our relationships. We expect once again to be enlightened so as to be able to continue to enlighten and what we iron out in our being will surely facilitate our ethical maturity and growth.

The divine realm, including its lord and master, is within and among us, so we surely have what it takes to predispose ourselves creatively, specifically, I suppose, by saying: "Yes, this is so. Let me know what is at stake and what is involved." I am human inasmuch as I take upon myself the responsibility for my actions and passions, for my opinions, feelings and humours and temperament. My humanity – at times, admittedly, of a precarious nature, such as when I try to make others responsible for my existence, and as I suppose it lets me down when in truth I neglect it – this humanity endows me with an easy, happy constitution and in exchange I provide a ready attentiveness and care. In terms of my humanity there is always a degree, at least, of give and take on my part. Really I should not think of myself, justly, as a human being until I have made my peace with that precondition of an exchange. Most important, causality does not come into it. What I give and what I take do not depend on each other, nor is the one influenced by the other. The simple fact of the matter is that both are ingredients of what we have a right to call humanity. When I say that neither of these two can influence the other I mean that we cannot repair a shortfall of ease and good fortune in our constitution by being more responsible, nor can we help a degree of irresponsibility by working towards greater constitutional ease and happiness. If we know ourselves to be burdened or in difficulties, on one side or from the other, let us take our eye off our humanity and tend to our divinity, for example to the quality of our residence in the divine realm – not as angels or demons, of course, but as human beings, capable of action and compassion.

Taking it from the other side now, let us assume we find that we lack clarity, certainty, confidence; that we feel alone, deserted, betrayed; that we are in a bad mood, ill-humoured, in ugly temper. We feel overexposed to painful influences, we suppose ourselves to be unjustly dealt with, unappreciated and impotent. This is not the time for us to insist on our divine origin, to celebrate, as it were, our detachment from the popular realm or to seek immunity and indifference by adopting a stance that would in our present case necessarily be ideal, angelic or righteous. Instead let us look to our humanity, to our willingness to suffer and our capacity for ethical behaviour, doing one another good. We are, proverbially, cast out of the divine realm merely on account of an emergent need for us to be human.

Equally we discover we cannot for the life of us cope with one another when its high time for us to recommit to our lord and to learn from our master.

Neither our humanity nor our divinity is ever utterly excluded from us but we can be wholly human and divine. That much, at least, we know now through knowledge of ourselves.

Being human, let me be ethical; being divine, let me be wise.

*

On the basis of what we have discovered so far, wisdom and ethical behaviour can go hand in hand, and when they do we have no complaints. We cheerfully manage a leisurely existence, attentive to our inward being and caringly disposed towards the world, while at the same time in tune with the divine realm and in touch with the one who orders that realm.

This is mistaken for an ideal state by those who suppose it might be prolonged or artificially sustained. As soon as we view it as a state however, as a static set of circumstances, it diminishes and disintegrates, for reasons we shall look at in a moment. What we tend to do then is, we either enlist our energy to come as close as possible to that state, always and again, after the manner of idealists, or we build a mythologic facsimile of it in the past, as the golden age, just for one example. We try to get 'back to nature', to imitate the noble savage, or we invent dynasties and yearn for the virtuous 'ancients' or strive to imitate antiquity, when 'all was well', or at least much better.

What idealists ignore is that human/divine beings need and want to grow. What we have described therefore is not a state but a process, and more specifically an organic process, involving work. For example, we increase our wisdom, or we lose it. Unless we become ever more ethical, we become more selfish. We grow to be more confident of else diffidence envelopes us. We continue to learn from our master or we mistake him for someone else, for an ideal or a myth. We become more caring and attentive or more absent minded and indifferent, and so on.

Only by continuing to know ourselves can we remain aware of our growth and of course of the impulses and stimuli that dictate and alter our growth. For example if we become distracted by external or internal accidents, such as chaotic energy or social superficialities, this is sooner of later brought to our intention by our indulgence in foolishness or a perpetration of harmful acts. At the beginning, however, this merely indicates for us that more or new growth is on the cards and that we would do well to behave accordingly. You might say we grow whether we know it or not but when we stop growing we soon know about it.

*

Not only are we human and divine but also mortal and immortal.

Take for example that tendency we have to inflate our worth, sometimes to the point where we have nothing but contempt for others. This is our mortality run riot. We forget that death is the only cure for extortionate demands we make on our biological system and on the world. Let us learn this once and for all, that we cannot court extinction with impunity. We may know all the physical laws since the Einsteinian revolution, but a moment of insight into ourselves can teach us that in spite of this, death is not mandatory and suddenly the lessons of a long life are marginalized.

Immortal we are due to our strivings for immortality but more importantly on account of our incorporation and embodiment of eternal life.

Here we have a concept, eternal life, that stems directly from our experience, that incomparable experience, of our body of knowledge, accessible to us by way of knowledge of ourselves. As our body of knowledge grows due to learning and teaching, we become increasingly familiar with eternal life, which we enjoyed, like wisdom, as little children and which, perhaps in spite of years of exposure to modern materialism and spiritualism, we may recover and accumulate in awareness.

I have written elsewhere in some detail about this new, invisible body of knowledge of ours and it remains here to stress the predilection of our body to participate in physical growth – mind, body and soul, while our ongoing knowledge of ourselves, which needs never even to pause, allows us to report on our progress in that department.

So for example we may set down the polarity of vitality and lethargy. Lethargy tells us that our body of knowledge is weakening and that we should, on that account, know ourselves much more diligently, while avoiding drugs of any and all description. A greater intensity of inward knowledge, which is knowledge of ourselves, will re-establish for us our connection with our body, so that we may recommence our affinity.

The question arises: Do we specifically know when our body is truly our own or are we only sensible to a loss of ownership, to which we may then respond in some ameliorative fashion?

What about vitality? Is it not a sign of body ownership?

Not really, for while lethargy informs us of a need for more intense, more concentrated inward knowledge, vitality is a cautionary experience. Vitality lets us know we are at risk and should see to our ambition, to our forward planning, to our aspiration towards future goals, for these, so we are being told, are no longer suitably anchored in our inward being, no longer properly connected to our body of knowledge while our peace of mind is in jeopardy.

So in the case of both lethargy and vitality we are in trouble, specifically with a view to our invisible body of inward knowledge and we may get back out of trouble by knowing, intensely or in leisurely fashion, this blessing of our body of knowledge.

We can, therefore, speak of a significant lethargy and a cautionary vitality. Lethargy calls for increased pressure on our nerves while vitality, endangering our sobriety, would make us more mindful of the fact that we are in the possession of our body of knowledge and therefore not to be swayed by mere 'adrenalin' sensation.

We are mortal inasmuch as we have what it takes to *die* readily *to* every influence adverse to our meaningful growth. We are also mortal in the sense that we will die if we do not take care to live. (By life, of course I mean eternal life and not internal or external survival.) There is the careless, accidental dying which is more or less culpable and the intentional 'dying to' some adverse influence, which is invigorating.

This knowledge of 'creative dying', as we might call it, is arrived at by us as soon as we have a firm hold on our immortality. We know how to 'die to' whatever would interrupt or corrupt our immortal integrity. This knowledge is then our first and foremost 'survival technique' in the divine realm. It stems from our communal agility in that realm, where we may always have before our eyes and within arm's reach this technique of dying to any and every potentially deadening influence. We withdraw whatever of us might be harmfully swayed and at the same time hand over whatever, presumably of ours, is of no benefit to us.

When we die to something we do not stop living eternal life and our body is not extinguished but safeguarded. We know how readily we become attached to things and how an aspect of our ethical behaviour is that doing good implies having felt not so good for a while. After all we are to remain accessible. Also, we may be assured that the divine realm is never overpopulated. It seems we must enter there first, before the human realm is properly revealed to us.

*

Also by way of knowing ourselves we learn that we are both wicked and virtuous. There is in truth as little contradiction here as in our being both mortal and immortal and being both human and divine. In all three cases, when there is a problem with this, we may confess that our eye, so to speak, is at fault and proceed towards a solution to the problem.

We are virtuous inasmuch as our present faculties are enlisted in the interest of contemporary communal welfare. We do ourselves good by doing others good. Communal welfare is experienced by all who espouse community rather than indulging in self. Also, this communal welfare must be contemporary and not modern or ancient. Always let the emphasis be on the here and now in the light of day.

Virtuously we develop our organs in line with our own original needs. Let each one see to this on his own behalf and not try to fall in with popular values. Really we can begin to be virtuous on the day of our birth, if nothing stands in our way. It is later in life that we can become consciously virtuous and intentionally virtuous.

Once again, we shouldn't imagine that our virtue depends on our avoidance of wickedness. It is human natural for us to behave virtuously and there is a distinct connection between our human natural and our virtuous behaviour. Our virtue depends on who we are and it demonstrates – we demonstrate in that way – our unique individuality. Therefore no two human beings can be virtuous in the same way.

We are not only wicked but bad as soon as we dance to the tune of some popular master. All popularity is bad but this is no reason for despair, since those who prefer the popular way, a the broad street along which the many trot to their destiny, do not necessarily interfere with those who prefer virtue unless the latter lack discipline. Then it can happen that the virtuous are challenged, so that they will show, will return to, their true colours.

So we say we are also wicked because we are always to some extent liable to return to, or to slide into, the ways of those who are ignorant of the virtuous way. Let us say it comes easy to us to behave virtuously, from our human nature, uniquely individual. Alas, our work takes us out of ourselves for we cannot get far unless we experiment, and before we know it we are no longer working in the interest of contemporary, communal welfare but instead we make selfish moves, we behave arrogantly, we do what we do in the dark. The fact that this is liable to happen to us points to our wickedness. Some suppose they cannot be wicked and they call themselves holy and therein lies their wickedness demonstrated. We do not perform wicked deeds but some of our thoughts and actions show we are wicked and there is really no need for this to be shown because we all know we are liable to behave carelessly and inconsiderately towards others, for example. So any morality that condemns certain predefined deeds or behaviour as wicked must be popular and cannot be of use to us.

*

It is due to our knowledge of ourselves that we are able to know anything else at all. As we know ourselves, we make room for world to impress us. You might say that by knowing ourselves we create the nerve capacity required for our recognition of beings. Things do not interest us in any case. If we cannot make them out we are none the poorer for it.

The transition from a codified environment, where things always mean the same – being things – to one of intimacy and spontaneity, where beings are themselves in ever new relations and affinities, is not a trivial matter that can be managed in terms of ambitious intellect. It is we ourselves, I and you, who play the deciding role, and the deciding factor is our unlimited personality. There is no end to the number of connections we can make between beings, ourselves included. The divine commonwealth originates in ourselves and in our community of being.

What a wonderful arrangement, that each and every one of us comes up with his or her own slant on world matters, so that we may communicate and enter upon rational reality!

25/06/10

* * * * *

* * *